China's Entry into the World Economy

CHINA'S ENTRY INTO THE WORLD ECONOMY

Implications for Northeast Asia and the United States

by Nicholas R. Lardy

THE
ASIA
SOCIETY

UNIVERSITY PRESS OF AMERICA

LANHAM • NEW YORK • LONDON

British Cataloging in Publication Information Available

Co-published by arrangement with
The Asia Society,
725 Park Avenue, New York, New York 10021

Library of Congress Cataloging-in-Publication Data

Lardy, Nicholas R.
   China's entry into the world economy.

   (Asian agenda report ; 11)
      1. China—Commerce—East Asia. 2. East Asia—
   Commerce—China. 3. China—Commerce—United States.
   4. United States—Commerce—China. 5. China—
   Commerce—Europe, Eastern. 6. Europe, Eastern—
   Commerce—United States. I. Title. II. Series.
   F3820.5.L37 1987   382'.0951   87-10625
   ISBN 0-8191-6371-6 (alk. paper
   ISBN 0-8191-6372-4 (pbk. alk. paper)

All University Press of America books are produced on acid-free
paper which exceeds the minimum standards set by the National
Historical Publication and Records Commission.

Contents

List of Tables

List of Figures

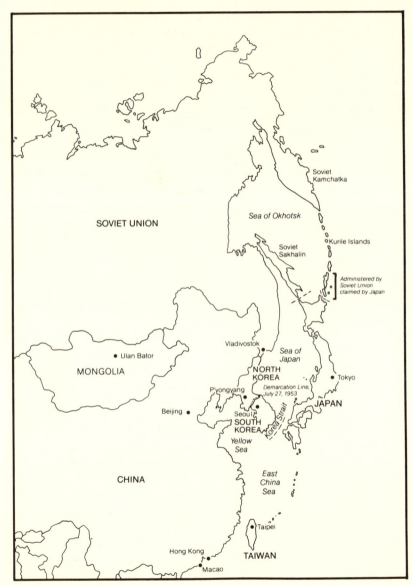

Northeast Asia

Foreword

In the years ahead Japan and the United States will face challenges to their interests and to their partnership in the Asian regional setting. How the two nations respond to changing conditions in the region will have significant consequences for other nations as well. The challenge is especially evident in Northeast Asia, where vital security interests of both nations are at stake and where economic relations are changing rapidly.

The Soviet military buildup in Northeast Asia, the confrontations on the Korean peninsula, the evolution of the Sino-Soviet relationship, and the Taiwan question make the security situation in the region one of the most sensitive and complex in the world. Political and security relations are further complicated by historic economic developments such as the opening and reform of China's economy, the emergence of Korea and Taiwan as major trading nations and competitors with Japan in some sectors, and the mounting pressure on Japan to reorient its economy. While most Americans and Japanese are focusing their attention on strains in their bilateral relationship, the potential for cooperation and conflict arising from these trends and issues has received relatively little notice. But successful management of U.S.-Japan interactions in Northeast Asia will require wider understanding in both countries.

This report is one result of a multiyear project sponsored by The Asia Society that seeks to stimulate greater American attention to U.S.-Japan interactions in Asia. The first phase of the project on "Japan, the United States and a Changing Asia" focused on Japanese and American interests and roles in Southeast Asia. It included an international conference in Japan in July 1984 that brought together more than fifty Americans, Japanese and Southeast Asians, a report authored by Charles Morrison of the East-West Center and published in the Asian Agenda report series, and a series of regional programs held in seven U.S. cities in February 1985.

The second phase of the project has examined the multilateral relations of Japan and the United States in Northeast Asia and has sought to stimulate wider discussion of them between Americans and Japanese and in the United States. In the fall of 1985 The Asia Society organized two study missions. The first, consisting of seven American specialists on Asian affairs, visited seven political and financial capitals of Northeast Asia to obtain the views of government officials, scholars, business people, educators and journalists on the international relations of the region. A second study team consisting of fifteen leaders from across the United States drawn from several professional fields visited Japan for a week of briefings and discusssions with Japanese officials, scholars and journalists on Northeast Asian affairs. A conference in Japan in November 1985 brought the two American teams together with Japanese counterparts for an exchange of views on the region.

This process of international dialogue provided the basis for an array of education outreach activities in the United States. These included lectures by the American specialists in different parts of the United States during the winter and spring of 1986, miniconferences in six American cities during May 1986 in which the American specialists and visiting Asian scholars discussed the region before diverse audiences, and a series of monographs by the American specialists on key topics relating to Japan and the United States in Northeast Asia. These monographs, including the present volume, are being published separately by The Asia Society in its Asian Agenda report series for wide distribution around the United States and Asia.

The specialist study mission was led by Professor Robert A. Scalapino of the University of California at Berkeley, one of the United States' leading authorities on Asian affairs. The other members included distinguished scholars representing different disciplines and area specialties: Herbert Ellison, an historian of Russia and the Soviet Union who was then director of the Kennan Institute of Advanced Russian Studies in Washington, D.C. and is now at the University of Washington, Seattle; Harry Harding, a political scientist specializing on China and Senior Fellow at the Brookings Institution; Donald Hellmann, a scholar of Japanese politics and foreign policy at the University of Washington, Seattle; Nicholas Lardy, a specialist on the Chinese economy also at the University of Washington, Seattle; Edward J. Lincoln, an economist working on Japan at the Brookings Institution; and myself (Marshall M. Bouton), representing The Asia Society.

Over a period of five weeks in October-November 1985 the Northeast Asian study mission visited Tokyo, Moscow, Ulan Bator, Beijing, Hong Kong, Taipei and Seoul. The mission also sought to visit Pyongyang but was not granted permission to do so by the North Korean authorities. In the course of its mission the American team met with over two hundred and fifty officials, scholars, journalists and business people. This intensive schedule of discussions was made possible through the generous assistance of host organizations in all seven cities: the Japan Center for International Exchange in Tokyo; the Institute of Oriental Studies in Moscow; the Executive Committee of the Union of Mongolian Organizations for Peace and Friendship with

Other Countries in Ulan Bator; the Chinese Academy of Social Sciences in Beijing; the Universities Service Center in Hong Kong; the Institute of International Relations in Taipei; and the Asiatic Research Center of Korea University in Seoul. The Asia Society is deeply grateful for this assistance.

This report is the latest in a series produced by The Asia Society's national public education program on contemporary Asian affairs, "America's Asian Agenda". The Asian Agenda program seeks to alert Americans to critical issues in Asian affairs and in U.S.-Asia relations, to illuminate the choices which public and private policy-makers face, and to strengthen transpacific dialogue on the issues. Through studies, national and international conferences, regional public programs in the United States, and corporate and media activities, the program involves American and Asian specialists and opinion-leaders in a far-reaching educational process. Asian Agenda publications emphasize short, timely reports aimed at a wide readership. Other recently published and forthcoming Asian Agenda reports address a variety of topics including Christianity in contemporary Korea, the United States and the ANZUS alliance, financing Asian growth and development, and the Philippines and the United States.

The Asia Society wishes to acknowledge the roles played by a number of individuals and organizations in the activities leading to this report. First, the Society is deeply indebted to Robert A. Scalapino for his extraordinary leadership of the American specialist mission to Northeast Asia. His exceptional knowledge, energy and goodwill were essential to the success of a complex and demanding endeavor. The Society is equally grateful to the other distinguished team members for their valuable contributions to the mission and other components of the project. Special thanks are also due to the leaders of the Asian organizations that arranged our programs: Tadashi Yamamoto, Evgenii Primakov, Luvsanchultem, Zhao Fusan, John Dolfin, Yu-Ming Shaw and Han Sung-Joo. We wish also to express deep appreciation to the many individuals in the cities visited who took time from their very busy schedules to talk with the team at length.

Major financial support for the project on "Japan, the United States and a Changing Northeast Asia" has been generously provided by the United States-Japan Foundation. The Japan-United States Friendship Commission made available monies for the U.S. regional programming of the project. Critical also was funding provided for the Society's Asian Agenda program by the Ford, Rockefeller and Henry Luce foundations and the Rockefeller Brothers Fund.

Finally, several members of the Society's staff were instrumental in the development of the project and the publications. John Bresnan assisted in the project's original overall design. Ernest Notar played an important early role in the project's phase on Northeast Asia. Most central to that second phase were Timothy J.C. O'Shea, who very ably organized all the project's activities, and Rose Wright, who provided excellent administrative assistance. Eileen D. Chang skillfully guided the publication of this and other reports emerging from the project, and Andrea Sokerka provided invaluable assistance.

Marshall M. Bouton
Director, Contemporary Affairs
The Asia Society
March, 1987

Preface

If one had to choose a single region of greatest importance to Americans in terms of their livelihood, political values and security, a leading candidate would be Northeast Asia. It is here that the most intensive economic interaction involving the United States will take place in the years immediately ahead, with interdependence—and the problems attendant to it—steadily advancing. It is here that the capacities of diverse societies to achieve and maintain a greater degree of political openness will be tested. And it is here that global and regional security issues are inextricably connected, with fateful consequences for all mankind.

In considering the future of Northeast Asia, one must juxtapose two equally important factors. On the one hand, each of the nation-states within the region bears a primary responsibility for the welfare of its own people, and the strength of its domestic political and social fabric. The decisions made by the leaders of each society are especially crucial at a time when virtually every government stands at a crossroads, facing the necessity of reconsidering past economic policies, political institutions and security strategies. Any attempt to shift the principal responsibility to external forces is fallacious.

At the same time, two nations—the United States and Japan—are deeply interrelated with both the developmental and security issues that confront the region as a whole. In their very dynamism, and the extraordinary reach of their power—economic, political or military—they cannot avoid exerting a major influence throughout Northeast Asia. Inaction as well as action sends its message, creates an impact. Their domestic policies no less than their foreign policies have far-reaching repercussions.

It thus seemed important and timely to undertake a study on United States and Japanese policies in a changing Northeast Asia. In liaison with knowledgeable Japanese, we set about examining our respective roles in the region—past, present and future.

Our task was to draw upon our background as students of Asia, supplementing this with a journey to all parts of the region available to us to hear the current ideas and proposals of Asians representing various political, economic and national perspectives. During the course of our five-week trip, we sought first to discern those indigenous elements of a geopolitical, ideological or economic nature that helped to shape a given society's attitudes and policies toward its neighbors, toward the region as a whole and especially toward the United States and Japan. We also explored the issues of greatest con-

cern to our respondents and their views as to the appropriate remedial action. At various points, attention focused upon the question of
American and Japanese policies, with an effort to examine viable
alternatives as well as the potentials that existed in current policies.

On occasion, as individuals we held different views from our Asian
or Soviet friends, either with respect to the relevant data or the conclu-
sions to be drawn from it. Being Americans, moreover, we sometimes
differed among ourselves. The monograph that follows, and the others in this series, thus represent the views of the author. No effort has
been made to achieve a complete consensus among us. Nevertheless,
those who read all of the monographs will discover a very considerable measure of agreement on most matters of consequence.

We are enormously grateful to those individuals and organizations
throughout Northeast Asia and in the Soviet Union who served as
hosts, facilitators, and discussants. To exchange views in a concentrated fashion, and to have the opportunity to compare and contrast
the views in one society with those in another over a very short period
of time proved both enlightening and stimulating.

On behalf of the group, let me also express our deep gratitude to
The Asia Society and its principal officers, especially Marshall Bouton, for making possible an experience that was both enriching and
enjoyable.

Robert A. Scalapino
Berkeley, California

Executive Summary

Since the mid-1970s China has embarked on a sweeping set of policy reforms that have simultaneously dramatically accelerated the pace of China's domestic economic development, more than quintupled China's total foreign trade, and led to an inflow of direct foreign investment surpassing that of any other developing country. China has thus begun to contribute in an important way to the economic ascendancy of the Pacific region in the world economy, an ascendancy evident in the patterns of growth of its national income and foreign trade and increased importance in world capital markets.

The resurgence of China's foreign trade has also reshaped economic relations within the Pacific region since a growing share of China's trade is intraregional. The growth of trade with Japan and Hong Kong is well known. But China has also initiated important trade relations with Taiwan and South Korea, and trade with the Soviet Union in recent years has grown more rapidly than any other bilateral relationship. In addition, although they are beyond the scope of this study, the opening of direct trade between China and Indonesia and China's rapidly growing trade with Singapore also form part of China's pattern of increasing intraregional trade.

While China's growing trade within Northeast Asia may contribute importantly to regional economic integration, important limits to that process are also evident. First, in the absence of political ties between China and the two smaller states in the region—Taiwan and South Korea, China's bilateral trade with these areas is both constrained to far less than its economic potential and is subject to considerable year to year instability. Similarly, although China's trade with the Soviet Union has been growing extraordinarily rapidly in recent years so that the Soviets now rank as China's fifth largest trading partner, the continuing frictions arising from large Soviet military deployments on China's borders, the continued Soviet occupation of Afghanistan, and ongoing Soviet support for Vietnamese expansion in Southeast Asia may ultimately constrain the bilateral trade and economic relationship.

Second, to date, the increasing relative importance of intraregional trade reflects the sum of the individual bilateral trade relationships in the region rather than the emergence of any institutional framework that would have regional economic integration as a goal. At the present time differences in underlying economic and political systems, large disparities in the levels of economic development among the nations of the region, and the lack of shared objectives

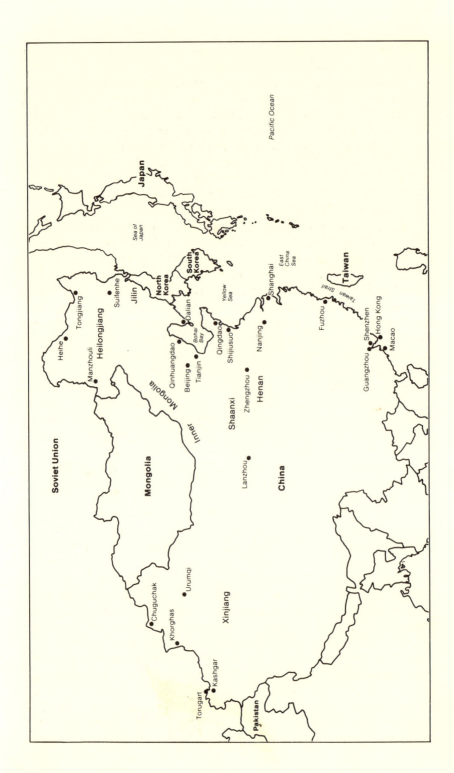

preclude the development of multilateral arrangements to facilitate greater regional economic integration.

Third, and finally, the process of increasing regional integration via trade may be constrained by factors internal to China. The rapid growth in China's trade was accompanied by unprecedentedly large deficits in both 1985 and again in 1986. These deficits were financed by drawing down previously accumulated reserves of hard currency, by increasing substantially foreign debt (estimated at almost 30 billion dollars at year-end 1986), by selling a billion or more dollars worth of nonmonetary gold on the London market in 1986, and by attracting large amounts of direct foreign investment. Each of these factors is not likely to continue in the future. China's foreign exchange reserves are, for practical purposes, virtually exhausted since they would be sufficient to finance only a few months worth of imports. In 1986 China, as part of a stand-by agreement with the International Monetary Fund, pledged to curtail substantially new borrowing from commercial banks, effectively limiting future credits to those that can be obtained from multilateral lending agencies such as the World Bank. Gold sales are limited by China's own domestic production and by the risk that larger sales would contribute to a softening of the price in the world market, undercutting the earnings flow. Finally, a sharp decline in contracted direct foreign investment in 1986, in response to the perception of increasing difficulties of operating joint ventures in China and the well publicized problems of several major joint ventures, may be a harbinger of future declines in the actual flow of direct foreign investment.

Thus unlike the last few years, China's future growth of imports will come to depend increasingly on its ability to sell its goods on the international market. While the degree of protection of labor intensive industries in the West will be an important determinant of the growth of Chinese exports, that growth also hinges critically on the success of urban industrial reforms. Since China's long term comparative advantage almost certainly lies in manufactured goods, the emergence of a dynamic export sector will depend on significant further reforms of China's still predominately state managed industry which has shown little sign of significant improvements in its efficiency since reform began. More satisfactory export performance will depend also on further changes in the foreign trade system as well as a commitment to move even further away from the goal of eventual self sufficiency that is still implicit in China's continuing policy of import substitution. Yet each of these changes has met with internal opposition, and it is not yet clear whether reforms in the industrial sector will be sufficiently successful to facilitate an improvement in China's export performance.

On balance these factors suggest a marked slowing in China's trade expansion in the years ahead. Moreover Japan will certainly remain the economic center of gravity in the region. Nonetheless China's trade will grow gradually and will be of increased importance to the United States because of expanded direct bilateral economic relations and because of Sino-U.S. competition in third country markets. But to date the United States has not formulated a coherent economic strategy to deal with the rise of China as a major participant in world markets. U.S. policy toward China has been variously formulated on the presumption that China is a potential counterweight to Soviet power in East Asia; a huge untapped market for U.S. goods and investment; a potential claimant on finite world resources; a socialist country that we might induce to enter the capitalist world; and, more recently as a nonmarket economy with substantial nontariff barriers to trade. Partly as a result of this inconsistency, U.S. trade with China has languished between 1981 and 1986 while China's total trade has soared.

While U.S. policy has been inconsistently formulated, Japan has developed an integrated economic strategy toward China that has led to major gains. Japan has long been China's major trading partner, but in the last five years China has grown increasingly more important in Japan's total trade. By 1985 China was Japan's second largest trading partner, ranking behind only the United States. Given its current lead and its far more significant efforts to understand China's foreign trade and domestic economy, Japan, not the United States, may continue to reap a major share of the benefits of China's growing international trade.

I. Introduction

In the 1980s the economic ascendancy of the Pacific region has received widespread recognition. The performance of the major economies in the region continues to be well above that achieved in either Europe or North America. Indeed, the relative performance of the East Asian region has probably improved since the oil price shocks of the 1970s. In the past decade the compound growth rate of Japan, Hong Kong, South Korea, Taiwan and Singapore has been fully three times the expansion achieved in France, Britain, West Germany, Italy and the Netherlands. Japan's relative growth performance has continued to be strong for so long that it has now surpassed the Soviet Union as the world's second largest economy. For the United States the dynamism of the region has been reflected in the rapid growth of transpacific trade in the past five years. In the early 1980s U.S. trade across the Pacific surpassed transatlantic trade, largely because of the dynamic growth of trade with East Asia. By 1984 trade with East Asian and Pacific countries accounted for almost one-third of total U.S. trade turnover.

While these developments are the result of trends that have been evident for more than two decades, the emergence of China as a more dynamic and more outwardly oriented economy has clearly accelerated and in some ways already begun to modify these patterns. Since the mid-1970s China has embarked on a sweeping set of policy reforms that have both dramatically accelerated the pace of China's domestic economic development and fundamentally transformed China's economic relations with the countries of Northeast Asia. The autarkic policies of the Maoist era have been abandoned, and China has begun a fundamental transformation toward a pattern of economic growth and development that has led to increasing integration with its neighbors in Northeast Asia and, to a lesser extent, the United States. The purpose of this monograph is to trace the origins of the transformation that is presently underway, to examine the prospects that it can be sustained, and to analyze the implications for U.S. policy in the region.

The central theme of this study is that China's new trade and investment policies have led to increased regional economic integration in Northeast Asia and have contributed to the overall economic dynamism of the Pacific region. But whether this trend will continue will depend both on the ultimate success of China's domestic economic reforms and the ability of countries in the region to mitigate

1

remaining political frictions. That is, China is unlikely to be able to continue to exhibit the rapid growth of trade of recent years in the absence of a more far-reaching reform in the modern industrial sector. A dynamic foreign trade sector cannot emerge and coexist with a centrally managed industrial sector that fails to exhibit significant positive productivity growth. Moreover, China's recent rapid growth of trade with Taiwan and South Korea, countries with which it has no diplomatic relations, and its rapidly growing trade with the Soviet Union, with which political relations remain strained, are unlikely to be sustained in the absence of progress toward a resolution of political differences.

II. The Economic Background

Except during the period of rapid growth of Sino-Soviet trade in the 1950s, China during the Maoist era pursued relatively autarkic trade and financial policies. During the 1960s, when the trade of both developing and industrialized economies was growing rapidly, China's trade was actually shrinking in real terms. Initially that was a response to the severing of the Sino-Soviet economic relationship and the collapse of the domestic economy as a result of the economically ill-fated strategy of the Great Leap Forward. But later, as domestic growth resumed, it reflected the autarky of the Cultural Revolution, when all but one of China's ambassadors were recalled from their posts and China turned inward. Similarly, while China in the 1950s had borrowed internationally, primarily from the Soviet Union, to help finance its domestic development program, in the 1960s it repaid all credits previously extended and pursued a policy of financial self-reliance.

The self-isolation began to break down beginning in 1971-1972 with the initiation of direct contacts between the United States and China. The trend toward opening to the outside world continued in 1975 when Zhou Enlai articulated a policy of comprehensive modernization of agriculture, industry, national defense and science and technology, a policy implicitly predicated on the acquisition of advanced Western technology. But despite some progress prior to Mao's death, foreign trade growth and liberalization of international financial policies were inhibited by the political instability brought on by the anticipation of the succession to Mao. In 1976 Deng Xiaoping, the driving force behind China's open door policy, was attacked and purged in part for his foreign trade and investment policies, and the reemergence of economic rationality was postponed until he was politically rehabilitated in mid-1977.

Since 1977, the year after Mao's death, China's international economic relations have been revolutionized and its trade has grown at an unprecedentedly rapid pace. As shown in Figure 1, between 1977 and 1985 total trade turnover (exports plus imports) rose from less than 15 billion U.S. dollars to almost 70 billion U.S. dollars, a fourfold increase. As a result China's position in the international trading system has advanced remarkably. Based on its exports China was the thirty-fourth ranked trading country in the world in 1976, but by 1985 China's exports were exceeded by only fourteen other countries. During this period China came abreast of the Soviet Union

CHINA'S FOREIGN TRADE 1976-1986
(Billions of U.S. $)

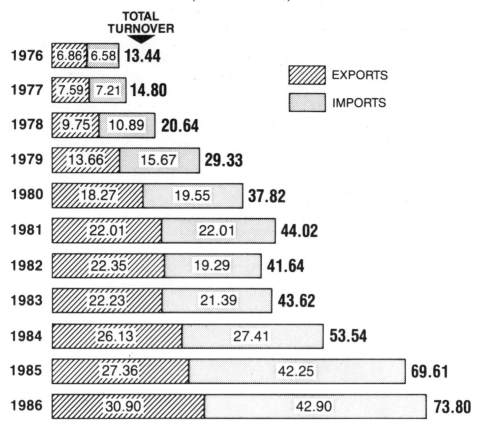

Figure 1

Note: Data for 1976-1980 are those released through the Ministry of Foreign Economic
Relations and Trade; for 1981-1986, through the Chinese Customs Administration.

Sources: State Statistical Bureau, *Chinese Statistical Yearbook* and *Annual Statistical Communique*, various years.

4

in its trade volume with market economies. By 1985 China's hard-currency trade was slightly larger than that of the Soviet Union.

At the same time as trade turnover grew rapidly, China's policy of financial self-reliance was abandoned. China has systematically joined each of the major international economic and financial organizations, beginning in 1980 with the World Bank and the International Monetary Fund (IMF). In 1984 China joined the Multifiber Arrangement, a textile trade monitoring body under the auspices of the General Agreement on Tariffs and Trade (GATT). As can be seen in Table 1, if China's 1986 application to resume its membership as an original signatory to the GATT is successful, China will join Yugoslavia, Romania and Hungary as the only socialist states belonging to all of the major international economic and financial organizations. In 1986 China also became a member of the Asian Development Bank, the only socialist country to belong to one of the major regional development banks. By the mid-1980s China had abandoned its earlier policy of financial self-reliance and had become the largest borrower from the World Bank, had successfully negotiated its first stand-by credit from the IMF and had, for the first time, begun to raise funds on the Eurodollar bond market.

Table 1
Socialist Country Memberships in International
Economic and Financial Organizations

International Monetary Fund	World Bank	General Agreement on Tariffs and Trade
Yugoslavia (1945)	Yugoslavia (1945)	Czechoslovakia (1947)
Romania (1972)	Romania (1972)	Cuba (1947)
China (1980)	China (1980)	Yugoslavia (1966)
Hungary (1982)	Hungary (1982)	Hungary (1973)
Poland (1986)		Poland (1967)
		China (1986)*

* formally applied for reinstatement of membership on July 11.

Sources: The World Bank Annual Report, various years; *International Monetary Fund Annual Report,* various years; and *GATT Activities,* various years.

The solicitation of direct foreign investment has been another dimension of the relaxation of financial self-reliance. Beginning in 1979 with the promulgation of a joint venture law in July and the establishment of special economic zones, China has issued an almost continuous stream of new laws and regulations that seek to attract direct foreign investment in a variety of forms. By the end of 1986 these efforts had attracted in excess of 8 billion U.S. dollars in foreign investment.

As China's international economic policies were altered, reforms in the domestic economy led to an acceleration of economic growth. Between 1978 and 1986 China's economy grew at an annual rate of more than 8 percent in real terms, a third higher than China's long-term, historic rate. More significantly, that rate put China well ahead of the performance over the same period of the Japanese economy and roughly on a par with the economies of Hong Kong, Singapore, Taiwan and South Korea. If China can sustain that relatively favorable performance vis-à-vis these historically most dynamic countries of East Asia it will transform the entire East Asian region.

The acceleration of China's growth and foreign trade has had a major effect on the patterns of trade within Northeast Asia. Japan is probably the most notable example. As shown in Table 2, in 1976 total bilateral trade was around 3 billion U.S. dollars and China was Japan's eighth largest trading partner, ranking behind the United States, Saudi Arabia, Australia, Canada, West Germany, the Soviet Union and the United Arab Emirates. By 1983 China was Japan's fifth largest, and by 1984 Japan's fourth largest, trading partner. In 1985 bilateral Sino-Japanese trade skyrocketed to over 16 billion U.S. dollars and China was Japan's second largest trading partner, ranking behind only the United States. Even though there was a downturn in Sino-Japanese trade in 1986 as China sought to reduce its trade deficit, China remained one of Japan's largest trading partner.

China's trade relations with Hong Kong have also been transformed. Traditionally Hong Kong has served as a distribution point for Chinese goods consumed by overseas Chinese in Southeast Asia. Thus there has been a large flow of foodstuffs and light manufactured goods exported through Hong Kong. But China was not a major market for goods produced in Hong Kong. Consequently Hong Kong traditionally registered a deficit in its trade with China. But the increased openness of the Chinese economy, including the development of four special economic zones on China's southeast coast, particularly Shenzhen and Zhuhai near Hong Kong and Macao, respectively, has fundamentally altered that traditional trade relationship. By 1985 China had emerged as Hong Kong's second largest export market and for the first time ever was able to export to

6

Table 2
China's Bilateral Trade with the Nations of Northeast Asia and the
United States, 1976-1986
(Millions of U.S. Dollars)

	Hong Kong	Japan	Mongolia	Soviet Union	North Korea	Taiwan*	United States	South Korea*
1976	1,787	3,039	1	415	395	40	317	—
1977	1,913	3,465	5	329	374	30	294	—
1978	2,533	4,824	6	437	454	50	992	—
1979	3,328	6,708	8	493	647	80	2,452	100
1980	4,353	9,201	7	492	678	320	4,811	200
1981	5,174	9,978	5	225	480	480	5,888	400
1982	4,977	8,761	5	276	545	300	5,336	300
1983	5,382	9,077	4	674	493	260	4,024	300
1984	8,954	12,728	5	1,183	500	550	5,960	700
1985	10,844	16,434	6	1,881	473	1,100	7,020	1,500
1986*	11,580	13,600	12	2,620	700	700	5,800	1,650

Notes: — negligible; * estimated. These data are compiled on a different basis from and thus are not directly comparable to the data for 1981-1986 shown in Table 2.

Source: Ministry of Foreign Economic Relations and Trade.

China as much as it imported. Bilateral trade volume grew another 20 percent in 1986, and Hong Kong experienced an unprecedented surplus in its trade with China. Even more surprisingly, in 1986 China replaced the United States as Hong Kong's biggest trading partner.

China's emerging trade relations with South Korea and Taiwan are perhaps even more striking, given the political difficulties that prevail in the bilateral relationships. Despite the firm resistance of Taiwan's ruling Nationalist Party to direct trade with the mainland, indirect trade via Hong Kong, and to a lesser extent via Singapore and other third countries, has burgeoned since the onset of economic reform in China. Bilateral trade via Hong Kong reached an all-time high of 1.1 billion U.S. dollars in 1985, and China ranked as Taiwan's fourth largest trading partner. If the burgeoning smuggling activities carried out across the Taiwan Straits were included, the volume of bilateral trade might be as much as twice that level according to some well-informed observers.

The expansion of China's trade with South Korea is subject to somewhat different constraints, but it is nonetheless growing rapidly.

The South Korean government has made no secret of its willingness to open formal diplomatic relations with China and develop direct trade ties. But the constraint is primarily on the Chinese side, which wishes to control the magnitude and visibility of its trade relationship with South Korea to avoid offending the North Koreans and perhaps push them toward an even closer relationship with the Soviet Union. Nonetheless in 1985 bilateral trade was estimated to approach 1.5 billion U.S. dollars, making China South Korea's fourth largest trading partner. More interestingly, as can be seen in Table 2, since 1984 China's trade with South Korea has far surpassed its trade with North Korea.

Finally, the absence of any significant progress toward resolving what the Chinese refer to as the three major obstacles to improved bilateral political relations with the Soviet Union (discussed further below) has not prevented significant changes in economic relations. Bilateral trade reached a post-1949 low of less than 50 million U.S. dollars in 1970 in the wake of the 1969 Chinese-Soviet military clashes along the Ussuri River and then rose to an average level of around 200 to 300 million U.S. dollars in the first half of the 1970s and 400 to 500 million in the second half of the decade. But since China rejected American attempts to develop closer strategic relations and moved toward a policy of equidistance between the Soviet Union and the United States in 1982, trade with the Soviet Union has multiplied rapidly. By 1985 bilateral trade rose to almost 2 billion U.S. dollars and the Soviet Union became China's sixth largest trading partner. In 1986 trade rose 40 percent over the previous year and exceeded 2.6 billion U.S. dollars, more than a tenfold increase over 1981. In 1986 the Soviet Union surpassed Singapore to become China's fifth largest trading partner. And a series of new agreements signed in 1985 and 1986 promised that trade will continue to grow rapidly in the years ahead.

China's trade with the states of Northeast Asia has shown only two exceptions—North Korea and Mongolia—to the pattern of dynamic growth discussed above. As shown in Table 2, bilateral Chinese-North Korean trade in 1981-1985 was about half a billion U.S. dollars, less than the level in 1979 and 1980, but appears to have increased in 1986.

Trade with Mongolia until 1986 had been on a plateau for a decade and remained extremely low, about 6 million U.S. dollars in 1985. Chinese exports consist primarily of silk and other textiles, light industrial goods, chemicals, machines and fruit; imports include timber and leather. The low level of bilateral trade reflects not only Mongolia's tiny population, 1.6 million in 1980, but also its extremely close ties to the Soviet Union and continuing Mongolian fears of Chinese territorial ambitions. Mongolian officials are apprehensive because China's post-Mao leadership has not refuted a purported statement by Mao that Mongolia is part of China, and they believe that the resurgence of national minorities research in China has as its objective proving that Mongolians were originally a Chinese nationality, that is, that they lived in China. Because of Mongolia's historically close ties to Moscow, more than 95 percent of its trade in recent years has been with members of the Council of Mutual Economic Assistance (CEMA), and the overwhelming share of this is with the Soviet Union.

But even Sino-Mongolian economic relations show signs of change. Bilateral negotiations on trade and related economic issues began in 1985 and led to the reopening of border trade and direct air service between Beijing and Ulan Bator, the Mongolian capital, ending a nineteen-year suspension of air service between the two countries. In August 1986 the two countries signed a consular treaty, the first since diplomatic relations were opened in 1949. These developments led to an acceleration of trade growth in 1986. Total bilateral trade turnover, estimated on the basis of trade flows during the first half of the year, at least doubled, with most of the increase due to increased Mongolian purchases of Chinese goods. It is likely that bilateral trade will continue to grow rapidly, as the opening of bilateral relations between Mongolia and the United States in 1987 probably indicates that Moscow has granted Ulan Bator slightly greater autonomy to determine its own foreign policy, including foreign economic relations. That should lead to a diversification in Mongolia's trade partners away from the pattern of the recent past of almost total dependence on the Soviet Union. Some indication of the potential growth is the fact that the level of Sino-Mongolian trade in 1985 was less than a tenth the average of the previous peak achieved in 1958-1962.

III. Sino-Japanese Economic Ties

Japan has been China's largest single trading partner for two decades, and the increasing importance and complexity of the bilateral economic relationship since China's adoption of the open door policy in the late 1970s is evident in several ways. Most significantly, the China market is of growing importance to Japanese firms, as reflected in China's rising rank among Japan's trading partners. Japan has long been China's top trading partner, but China became one of Japan's most important trading partners only in recent years, rising to number two in 1985. Put alternatively, a decade ago it was commonly argued that as China's trade grew, Japan's dominant position in the China market would erode. But this has not happened. China's total trade has soared, but Japan has retained its market share, the bilateral trade volume has become large in absolute terms, and the gap between the volume of Sino-Japanese trade and trade between China and other partners has grown.

Second, Japan has become the largest national supplier of aid to China. Through its Overseas Economic Cooperation Fund (OECF), Japan in two development loan packages in 1979 and 1984 committed more than 3.5 billion U.S. dollars to aid various construction projects, projects that already have had and will continue to have a positive effect on the bilateral trade relationship. The most obvious examples are Japanese support for rail line and port improvements that will increase China's ability to export more coal and petroleum to Japan. In 1983, for example, a 7.6 billion yen loan was extended for the electrification of the Baoji (Shaanxi) to Zhengzhou (Henan) rail line, substantially increasing the carrying capacity of the rail system leading out of Shaanxi province, where almost half of China's coal is mined. The terms of the loan are extremely generous compared to normal commercial credit. The repayment period is thirty years with a ten-year grace period, meaning the repayments will not begin until the mid-1990s, and the interest rate is only 3.25 percent per annum. In terms of their grant component these loans approach those made by the International Development Association of the World Bank, generally considered to be the most favorable source of long-term economic development credits. Earlier OECF financial commitments were made for port development at Shijiusuo, improvements of the Yanzhou-Shijiusuo rail line, and the Beijing-Qinhuangdao rail line.

Japan's aid program contributes to increased bilateral trade for two reasons. First, although the loans are untied and thus in principle can be used by the Chinese to finance the procurement of project-related equipment, supplies and consulting and engineering services from any country, the Chinese utilize about three-quarters of the funds to purchase equipment, facilities and services from Japan. Second, the projects funded by OECF are all designed to facilitate the flow of Chinese exports to Japan. Almost half of Japan's imports from China consist of crude oil, petroleum products and coal. The port and rail development projects supported by OECF loans will facilitate both the domestic transport of these commodities to major Chinese ports and the loading of the goods in the ports.

The third manifestation of the increasing complexity of the bilateral Sino-Japanese economic relation is in credit markets. Through several channels Japan has become the most important international financial market for China. Japanese Export-Import Bank credits of about 2 billion U.S. dollars were extended in 1979 to finance the development of energy resources in China. These loans were for fifteen years with an annual interest rate of 6.25 percent.

The Chinese have also raised substantial funds in the Japanese bond market. From late 1981 through 1986 various Chinese borrowers floated eleven bond issues in the Japanese market. As shown in Table 3, the issuers include the Bank of China, the China International Trust and Investment Company (CITIC) and two of the provincial branches of CITIC, the Fujian Investment and Enterprise Corporation (FIEC) and the Shanghai Investment and Trust Corporation (SITCO).

Cumulatively, through 1986, China had borrowed the equivalent of almost 2 billion U.S. dollars on international bond markets, the great majority in Japan. And, for reasons discussed below, even though China made its first offering on the Eurodollar bond market in 1986, Japan is likely to remain a critical market for most Chinese issues of international bonds. Finally, Japanese banks have been major suppliers of commercial credit to China.

These developments in trade, aid and borrowing are all the more remarkable since Sino-Japanese relations have been marked by substantial frictions. In early 1979 the Chinese unilaterally suspended contracts of about 2.5 billion U.S. dollars for purchase of industrial plants, cancellations that became known in Japanese industrial circles as the "China shock." Again in 1981 the Chinese canceled 1.5 billion U.S. dollars in contracts for Japanese plants, primarily in the fields of steel and petrochemicals. Many of these projects were later revived, but only after the Japanese side agreed to supply additional financial credits.

On the other side of the equation the Chinese have had their own complaints. In 1985, for example, Chinese officials complained of Japan's reluctance to undertake major direct investments in China and of the substantial imbalance in favor of Japan in the bilateral trade

11

relationship. They also protested the visit of the Japanese prime minister to the Yasukuni Shrine, where Japanese war criminals are buried. The Chinese have protested, first in 1982 and again in 1986, the treatment of the Sino-Japanese War in government-approved school textbooks.

Table 3
Chinese Sales of Bonds on International Markets, 1981-1986

Year	Chinese issuer	Nature of placement/lead underwriter	Amount	Market
1981	CITIC	Private	10 billion yen	Japan
1983	FIEC	Private	5 billion yen	Japan
1984	Bank of China	Public/Nomura securities	20 billion yen	Japan
1985	CITIC	Public/Daiwa Securities	30 billion yen	Japan
1985	Bank of China	Public/Nomura	20 billion yen	Japan
1985	Bank of China	Public/Deutsche Bank	150 million DM	Germany
1985	CITIC	Private	300 million HK $	Hong Kong
1985	Bank of China	Public/Nomura	150 million US $	Japan
1985	Bank of China	Public/Nomura	30 billion yen	Japan
1985	CITIC	Public/Deutsche Bank	150 million DM	Germany
1985	FIEC	Public/Nomura Securities	10 billion yen	Japan
1985	CITIC	Public/Yamaichi Securities	100 million US $	Japan
1986	CITIC	Public	40 billion yen	Japan
1986	SITCO	Public	10 billion yen	Japan
1986	Bank of China	Public/Deutsche Bank	200 million US $	Europe
1986	CITIC	Public	400 million HK $	Hong Kong
1986	FIEC	Public/Nomura	50 million US $	Singapore

Sources: China Business Review, various issues, and the international financial press.

Chinese complaints concerning the economic aspects of the bilateral relationship appear to have some merit. Despite Japan's persistent dominant role in trade with China, total Japanese investment in China is miniscule not only relative to Japan's overall investment abroad but also relative to total foreign investment in China. Of total investment in China of about 5.4 billion U.S. dollars at the end of the third quarter of 1985, only about 2 percent was Japanese. And Japanese investment in China in 1985 comprised only about 1 percent of Japanese investment abroad.

Despite persistent official Chinese complaints over a period of several years, there is little prospect that this situation will change in the short run. While other Western firms rushed to initiate joint ventures and subsequently discovered that conditions were far from propitious, Japanese firms, guided by Japan's Ministry of International Trade and Industry, have by and large taken a cautious approach. The bilateral trade balance has also moved in Japan's favor since 1983. By 1985 the Chinese deficit in trade with Japan had reached an unprecedented level of 5.2 billion U.S. dollars. On a customs clearance basis the deficit was even greater, almost 9 billion U.S. dollars. Despite regular high-level consultations on the trade imbalance, there is little evidence of Japanese response to Chinese pleadings that Japan increase its purchase of Chinese goods. The lack of a significant response by the Japanese and the declining value of China's petroleum sales to Japan meant there was only a slight drop in the 1986 bilateral trade deficit, even though China cut its purchases of Japanese goods by almost one-fourth.

IV. Emerging Relations with the Soviet Union and Eastern Europe

The Chinese have long said that there can be no significant improvement in Sino-Soviet relations without some progress toward resolving what they label the three fundamental obstacles: the massive presence of Soviet troops on the border with China; the Soviet military intervention in Afghanistan; and Soviet support for Vietnamese expansion in Southeast Asia. Despite the lack of significant Soviet concessions on these issues, economic relations have improved dramatically in recent years and show every sign of continuing to flourish. The increase in the bilateral trade volume, noted at the outset of this study, has occurred in a broader framework of steadily improving state-to-state relations.

The turning point came in the fall of 1982, when after a several-year pause, the Chinese and the Soviets resumed their long-stalled deputy ministerial level talks between Leonid Ilyichev and Qian Qichen. As alluded to earlier, the opening primarily reflected the decision by the Chinese to adapt a somewhat more equidistant posture between the two superpowers. The first round of discussions established the principle of biannual talks with one round of discussions in each capital.

While the communiques of the initial rounds of the formal talks did not indicate any progress on major political issues, indirectly the negotiations led quickly to significant progress on economic issues. Shortly after the second round of talks in the spring of 1983, both sides announced that border trade, which had been suspended since 1962, would resume. In 1984 the Chinese announced the expansion of rail-loading facilities in Heilongjiang province and the Inner Mongolian Autonomous Region to facilitate the expanded flow of goods between China and the Soviet Union. At the end of the year, at the conclusion of talks between Ivan V. Arkhipov, Soviet first deputy prime minister, and Yao Yilin, a Chinese deputy prime minister, the two countries signed agreements covering economic and scientific and technical cooperation.

The most important feature of the agreements was the Soviet commitment to provide extensive technical and other assistance to upgrade seventeen major Chinese industrial plants that were among the much larger number of projects built with Soviet assistance in the 1950s. The Soviets also agreed to assist in building seven entirely new plants in China. The two socialist states have also agreed to hold annual trade exhibitions in each other's capital through 1990. The first Chinese trade exhibit since 1953 was held in Moscow in July and August 1986, and the first Soviet industrial and trade exhibit in Beijing was in late 1986.

The talks with First Deputy Prime Minister Arkhipov, who is an alternate member of the Soviet Politburo and the highest ranking Soviet visitor to China since 1969, were said to be particularly warm. He was personally greeted by senior Chinese Politburo members who worked with him in the 1950s when he was the chief of the Soviet technical assistance program for China.

Within months of the Arkhipov-Yao Yilin talks in Beijing, Yao Yilin flew to Moscow to sign a five-year trade and economic agreement that called for more than tripling bilateral trade during the period 1986-1990 as compared with 1981-1985. Cumulative trade would be almost 36 billion Swiss francs (about 14 billion U.S. dollars) as compared with 9.8 billion Swiss francs in the earlier period.

Moreover, according to Soviet sources, on the occasion of a visit to Beijing in the fall of 1986 by Soviet First Vice-Premier Nikolay Talyzin, who is also head of the Soviet economic planning agency, Gosplan, a new trade agreement was signed calling for even higher levels of bilateral exchange. Unfortunately the new agreement has not been published, and its provisions are unclear. One Soviet source suggested that bilateral trade would reach 7.5 billion U.S. dollars in 1990, a sharp increase from the 3.5 billion U.S. dollar level envisaged in the agreement signed in 1985. Similarly, an English-language Chinese paper less than two months after the conclusion the Talyzin visit stated that cumulative Sino-Soviet trade in 1986-1990 would reach 30 billion U.S. dollars, more than double the cumulative 14 billion U.S. dollar figure announced after the Arkhipov-Yao talks in Moscow in 1985. Finally, some sources have suggested that in Talyzin's meetings with high-ranking Chinese officials he also committed the Soviet Union to offer financial credit for China's development program. The full scope of the new agreement may be made public after the second session of the Sino-Soviet Commission for Trade and Economic Cooperation, which will meet in Moscow in 1987.

In the late summer of 1986 both sides also agreed to open new consular offices. The Soviet consular office in Shanghai, closed since 1962, reopened in December 1986. The first Chinese office opened in Leningrad in November. The Chinese have agreed to an additional Soviet consulate in Harbin, and the Soviets have reportedly requested permission to open additional consulates in Shenyang, Nanjing, Guangzhou and Urumqi.

In the late fall, only a few months after the possibility was first mentioned by Soviet leader Gorbachev, the two countries also agreed to establish a committee to draft a comprehensive plan to develop the water resources of the Amur and Argun Rivers which demark the greater part of the boundary between China and the Soviet Union east of Mongolia. While the details have not been released, both sides have agreed to multi-purpose development of the two rivers, including power generation, flood prevention, navigation and water utilization. Interestingly the agreement for cooperative development effectively revives an agreement first reached in 1956. Although that agreement led to a joint Sino-Soviet survey of the region and some preliminary meetings, the agreement was not implemented as Sino-Soviet relations worsened during the Great Leap Forward, leading to the open split of 1960.

In February 1987 China and the Soviet Union reopened in Moscow their negotiations on the demarcation of their border along the Amur and Ussuri Rivers. The impetus for reopening the talks, after a lapse of almost nine years, was Gorbachev's July 1986 speech in Vladivostok. In that speech Gorbachev gave up the long-time Soviet position that the border ran along the Chinese shore of the Amur River and accepted the longstanding Chinese position that the border runs down the main channel. Some speculate that during the border talks the Soviets will make a further concession with respect to the Ussuri.

In addition to the new program of technical cooperation, the five-year trade agreement, reciprocal trade fairs, the consular agreement, the committee to oversee a TVA-type development in the Amur River basin and the opening of border talks after a hiatus of about nine years, other indications suggest that economic relations will continue to improve and bilateral trade will continue to expand. First, under the policies of decentralization in which trade authority in China has devolved to provincial and lower levels of government administration, provincial and regional officials in both northeastern and northwestern China have rapidly promoted trade with the Soviet Union. Most notable is the reopening of border trade, locally approved trade that takes place outside the formal bilateral state-to-state trade agreements. Border trade between the Soviet Union and the provincial-level administrations of Heilongjiang, Inner Mongolia and Xinjiang began in 1983. Discussions were underway in late 1986 that would also open border trade between Jilin province and the Soviet maritime provinces. As Table 4 indicates, the number of Chinese cities that have been opened to border trade has grown steadily since 1982. The volume of such trade has grown rapidly, more than quadrupling in 1984 to reach well over 100 million U.S. dollars. Since the trade appears to meet long felt needs of the local populations on both sides, it is likely to grow rapidly.

16

Second, Chinese national policy at present encourages the Western economic orientation of provinces in the Northwest, such as Xinjiang. Hu Yaobang, while he was the Chinese Communist Party general secretary, for example, twice visited Xinjiang and encouraged the region to develop trade ties with western Asia, including Pakistan and Middle Eastern countries, as well as the Soviet Union.

Table 4
Chinese Cities Open to Border Trade with the Soviet Union

Province	City	Year opened
Heilongjiang	Suifenhe	1983
	Heihe	1985
	Tongjiang Port	1986
Inner Mongolia	Manzhouli	1983
Xinjiang	Khorghas	1983
	Torugart	1983
	Chuguchak	1985

Sources: Reports of the Chinese news agency, *Xinhua,* appearing in numerous official publications.

Major new investments in transport infrastructure have been and are being made to facilitate the trade flows between these regions and adjacent states. The 1,892-kilometer Lanzhou-Urumqi rail line, which first linked Xinjiang with the rest of China in 1962, is now undergoing major renovation. The initial southern extension of the Lanzhou-Urumqi rail line opened in 1984, running from Turfan to Korla, and has recently been extended over one thousand kilometers to Kashgar in southwestern Xinjiang. From there the Karakoram Highway crossing the mountains to Pakistan was constructed and opened to traffic in May 1985. Already this road from Kashgar to the Kunjirap Pass on the Pakistani border is scheduled for resurfacing and upgrading, using funds provided by the central government.

The Chinese also decided in recent years to extend the Lanzhou-Urumqi rail line west to the Soviet Union to join a main Soviet east-west line at Alma Alta. When completed the line will be the first international rail link in China's far Northwest. The work on the first 240 kilometers, from Urumqi to Wusu, began in May 1985. The priority assigned to the completion of the project is suggested by Chinese claims that the speed of construction in the first five months surpassed that of all rail lines constructed in China since 1949.

Completion of the first segment to Wusu will be in October 1987 and will be followed by the second phase, which will extend the line to the Soviet border. Mr. Gorbachev in his July 1986 speech alluded to a Chinese request for Soviet assistance in the second phase of the rail project, a request he predicted would receive a positive response.

The extension of the Lanzhou-Urumqi line will facilitate increased trade not only with the Soviet Union, but also with Central Asia, the Middle East and Europe since the line will form a land bridge linking the port of Dalian in the Northeast with Amsterdam. Compared to the sea route through the Suez Canal, the transport cost and time savings are estimated at 30 and 50 percent, respectively. The line is expected to facilitate the flow of goods from Japan and Southeast Asia through China to Europe, increasing Chinese earnings in their international services account.

International air service from the Northwest is also being established. In 1986, the Chinese Civil Aviation Administration announced the opening of service from Urumqi, the capital of Xinjiang, to Addis Ababa, the capital of Ethiopia. A new Xinjiang regional aviation company, Xinjiang Airline, has been established and four regional airports, including one at Hotan, have been expanded and upgraded to open local air service to Pakistan and the Soviet Union, using four TU-154 medium-range jet aircraft purchased from the Soviet Union.

Third, improved relations with the Soviet Union are an integral part of the open door policy. Japanese and Westerners commonly assume that the open door policy means opening to market-oriented economies, but the Chinese now are quick to state that opening includes increased trade with socialist economies as well as with the West. That perspective is reflected not only with close economic ties with the Soviet Union but also with Eastern Europe. In 1985 China signed, for the first time, five-year trade agreements with East Germany, Poland, Hungary, Czechoslovakia and Bulgaria and scheduled major trade exhibits in East Germany and Hungary. Trade ties with Rumania and Yugoslavia, which have traditionally benefited from China's closer political ties with those nations, have also been strengthened through long-term trade agreements. These agreements have led to significant trade growth. In 1986, when China's total trade grew only 5 percent, trade with five Eastern European countries rose by 75 percent to 2.5 billion U.S. dollars.

Fourth, for both countries trade is conducted on what both sides refer to as a "goods exchange" or barter basis, obviating the need to utilize scarce foreign exchange. As both countries have experienced some difficulty in expanding their exports to market economies in recent years, that feature of the trade is perceived by both sides as offering some advantage.

Fifth, there is an underlying economic rationale to China's expanding trade and economic relations with the Soviet Union and Eastern Europe. It is sometimes argued that the trade patterns of China and the Soviet Union are more competitive than complementary and do not form the basis of a substantial bilateral trade relationship. In this view, since there is a certain similarity in the import and export commodities of each country, trade will be limited. They both, for example, have exported petroleum and petroleum products and imported foodgrains. Moreover, the Soviet Union will not be able to supply China with the high-technology goods essential to China's ambitious modernization program, and there is a paucity of important Chinese exports that would find a market in the Soviet Union.

But this argument about lack of complementarity overlooks the fact that China imports large quantities of raw materials, standard industrial products such as steel and many manufactured goods, such as electric power generating equipment, that are characterized by a relatively low level of technological sophistication. Thus the Soviet Union and Eastern European countries supply growing volumes of critical commodities to China, notably timber, pig iron, rolled steel, trucks, automobiles, electrical equipment, chemical fertilizer, cement and even consumer durables in short supply in China such as motorcycles, refrigerators and washing machines. Moreover, the Chinese purchase other, more sophisticated equipment and machinery such as diesel locomotives, jet aircraft, major equipment and material for 500-kilovolt transmissions lines and associated power substations because of the presumed price advantage.

Finally, to upgrade the plants built with extensive Soviet assistance in the 1950s the Chinese need machinery and parts that simply are not available from other sources of supply.

On the other side of the trade equation the Soviet Union and Eastern Europe can serve as an important market for Chinese goods, some of which face increased barriers in Western markets. For example, the Soviet Union is an increasingly important market for Chinese textile products. In 1985 the Chinese exported about 600 million U.S. dollars worth of cotton cloth, garments and cotton to the Soviet Union and Eastern European countries, a 60 percent increase over 1984. Indeed, as rising protectionism in textiles has curtailed the growth of Chinese exports to market economies, the development of the Eastern European and Soviet markets has been increasingly important. The expansion of the market for textiles in the socialist countries in 1985 largely compensated for the fall in sales to market economies, allowing China's total textile export volume to remain constant.

19

Similarly, the Soviet Union is a growing market for Chinese agricultural exports, including meat, processed foods, fruits, foodgrains, peanuts and soybeans, and for light industrial goods, primarily consumer goods such as handicrafts, thermos flasks, flashlights and other household articles. There is no reason to presume that this mutually profitable bilateral trade flow will not continue to grow in the future.

Beyond the increased flow of goods and of technical assistance, the Sino-Soviet economic relationship may expand to include a Chinese role in developing the vast mineral and forest resources of Siberia. A large share of the natural resources, particularly the energy, needed for future Soviet growth lies to the east of the European industrialized Russian heartland. Gorbachev's July 1986 speech calling for accelerated development of the Soviet Far East is only the most recent acknowledgement of the vast long-term potential contribution of Siberian resources to Soviet economic growth.

But the Soviets have been notoriously unsuccessful in encouraging migration to these regions, and as long ago as the 1950s they expressed an interest in utilizing Chinese labor to exploit Siberian resources. Although the prospective cooperation in the Khrushchev era was aborted by the Soviet withdrawal of technical assistance from China in mid-1960, according to some reports Khrushchev's successors have revived the discussion by requesting that the Chinese supply labor to assist in Siberian development. In an interview after the conclusion of his September 1986 visit to China, Soviet First Vice Premier Talyzin alluded to this, saying that China and the Soviet Union "will adopt new measures of cooperation based on production and utilization of natural resources." And some Chinese officials seem ready to pursue this option as a means of paying for increased imports of Soviet raw materials, notably timber. This would put China in a position similar to the North Korean government, which also supplies labor for Siberian projects in exchange for raw materials such as timber.

In Beijing officials who are not committed to the primacy of the Chinese relationship with the United States even speak of a possible trilateral form of cooperation in Siberia involving Soviet resources, Japanese capital and Chinese labor. This is a rather remarkable development considering that the Chinese in the mid-1970s brought pressure to bear against the Japanese when they were considering Moscow's invitation to participate in several Siberian development projects, notably a combined pipeline-railroad to ship Siberian petroleum west to Soviet Pacific ports.

V. Commercial Relations with the United States

Unlike Japan, which pursued a policy of unofficial trade relations prior to the normalization of relations in the early 1970s, the United States had no trade relationship with China until 1972. Following the initiation of official, direct Sino-American contacts in 1971-1972, the institutional framework to facilitate trade developed rapidly. The United States lifted its embargo on commercial relations with China in mid-1971 and, after formal diplomatic relations were established in 1978, a bilateral trade agreement was signed in 1979. Shortly thereafter the United States granted China most-favored-nation (MFN) status, access to the export credit facilities of the United States Export-Import Bank (Eximbank), eligibility for technical assistance from U.S. government agencies such as the United States Army Corps of Engineers on a compensatory basis and eligibility for the operations of the United States Overseas Private Investment Corporation (OPIC). As can be seen in Table 5, China thus joined a select group of socialist countries that had been granted MFN status.

U.S. Export Controls

As the trade relationship developed, controls on U.S. exports to China have been repeatedly relaxed. Beginning with the Korean War, controls on U.S. exports to China were more severe and included more items than the restrictions imposed on exports to the Soviet Union. That so-called China differential was not lifted until the United States formally ended the trade embargo in mid-1971. Between 1971 and 1981 China fell into country group Y and was subject to the same restrictions as the members of the Warsaw Pact, but more relaxed than country group Z, which at that time included Cuba, North Vietnam and North Korea. In the spring of 1981 China was shifted to a unique country category P, which allowed for a reverse differential in favor of U.S. exports to China relative to the Soviet Union and other countries of the Warsaw Pact. Under these arrangements the Office of Export Administration was given increased latitude in approving validated licenses for the export of products and technical data controlled on national security grounds, particularly so-called dual-use technology. More recently, in a further liberalization of technology transfer policy in May 1983, President Reagan announced that since China was a "friendly nonallied country" it would be shifted to country group V, along with most of our Western European allies and other friendly nonallied nations.

Table 5
Socialist Countries with United States
Most-Favored-Nation Status

Country	Year granted
Yugoslavia	1948
Poland	1960
Romania	1975
Hungary	1978
People's Republic of China	1980

Note: Imports from countries with most-favored-nation (MFN) status are dutiable at the lowest tariff rates applied to imports into the United States, rates negotiated within the framework of the General Agreement on Tariffs and Trade (GATT).

The MFN status of Poland, Romania, Hungary and the People's Republic of China is subject to annual renewal by the president in accordance with the Jackson-Vanik Amendment (Section 402) to the Trade Act of 1974. The amendment links MFN status, credits from the U.S. government and other benefits to emigration policies for those nonmarket economies that did not already enjoy MFN status at the time the act was passed. Under these review provisions Poland's MFN status was suspended from November 1982 until February 1987.

Sources: U.S. International Trade Commission, *Tariff Schedules of the United States (Annotated)*, various years.

As is evident in Table 2, bilateral Sino-American trade has grown rapidly during this period. Total trade turnover reached 7 billion U.S. dollars in 1985, almost three times the level of 1979, the last year trade was conducted without the benefit of MFN status for China. The United States has remained China's third largest trading partner, after Japan and Hong Kong.

Despite this growth, the bilateral economic relationship with China is far less important to the United States than to Japan. Whereas China was Japan's second largest trading partner in 1985, U.S. trade with China was still miniscule relative to total U.S. trade. Even in 1985, when bilateral Sino-American trade reached an all time high, China was only sixteenth among U.S. trading partners, ranking behind Canada, Japan, Mexico, all of our major trade partners in Western Europe as well as South Korea, Taiwan, Singapore, Hong Kong, Brazil and Venezuela. Its rank slipped even lower in 1986 when Sino-U.S. trade was off 15 percent.

The reasons for this lag in the bilateral trade volume are poorly understood but clearly include U.S. controls on exports of high technology products to China; United States import restrictions on Chinese goods; the failure of the United States to extend the benefits of the generalized system of preferences to Chinese sales in the American market; and the absence of any bilateral program providing U.S. aid or subsidized credits to China.

Many American firms feel that the implementation of export control regulations impedes the flow of U.S. high-technology products to China. Presidential orders may shift China from a more to a less restrictive country group category, but lower-level government bureaucrats are said effectively to sabotage these rulings by subjecting exports to the older, more stringent requirements. Particularly in 1983, when China was shifted to country group V, officials in the Office of Export Administration continued to subject license applications to detailed interagency reviews leading to lengthy delays.

Moreover, even after they are licensed by the U.S. government many products must be submitted for the approval of the Coordinating Committee for Multilateral Export Controls (COCOM) a Paris-based international agency established by the major Western industrialized countries in 1949 to control the export of military-related technologies to communist countries. Since the United States maintains a substantial comparative advantage in those product areas, the controls have a particularly inhibiting effect on U.S. trade with China. Moreover, because the United States has sought to utilize the COCOM system of controls to impose more restrictive controls on exports to the Soviet Union than is desired by Japan and most of the countries of Western Europe, successive U.S. administrations have been exceedingly cautious in trying to liberalize the implementation of COCOM regulations as they apply to China. The result has been that bilateral U.S.-China trade has been indirectly inhibited by U.S. policy toward the Soviet Union.

U.S. Import Barriers

While export controls have held down U.S. sales to China, import restrictions have slowed the growth of Chinese sales in the United States. While Chinese sales to Japan of cotton and textile products have been growing at well over 20 percent annually since 1981, Chinese sales of cotton textiles in the U.S. market have been restrained by quotas imposed unilaterally on a growing number of product categories. When the first textile agreement with China was reached in 1980, the United States imposed quantitative restrictions on only eight separate categories of textile goods. The scope of restrictions has expanded continuously since then, and by 1986, 90 percent of Chinese textile products sold in the U.S. market were subject to controls.

The Multi-Fiber Agreement (MFA) adopted by the GATT in mid-1986 extends MFA to include ramie and flax. In the first half of the 1980s Chinese exports of these uncontrolled fibers to the United States skyrocketed. Sales of ramie, for example, reached a level of more than five hundred million square yards, mostly in the form of sweaters. The new MFA means the United States can now negotiate restrictions on ramie fiber sales in the U.S. market and thus promises to be even more constraining than in the past. In negotiations in the late fall of 1986 the United States sought Chinese agreement to restrict increases of Chinese ramie exports to a modest rate of growth, reportedly in the range of from 5 to 10 percent annually, far less than the double-digit growth of previous years. The Chinese refused to agree to these restrictions and broke off the talks. Moreover, the Chinese have thus far refused to sign the new MFA. The U.S. view is that the refusal of the Chinese to sign the new agreement does not impinge on the legality, under the GATT charter, of the United States imposing quota restraints unilaterally. In early 1987 quotas were imposed for the first time on six categories of ramie and ramie-blend fibers.

Chinese reaction to these restrictions has been sharp. They have protested protectionism; imposed (in 1983) an embargo on U.S. sales of cotton, synthetic fibers, soybeans and wheat; organized with other textile-exporting nations an International Textile and Clothing Bureau to lobby for less restrictive trade practices both in Europe and the United States; and continuously requested the removal of all COCOM restrictions on the flow of U.S. technology to China.

Finally, Japan and some other industrialized countries, notably members of the European Economic Community, Switzerland and Australia, since the late 1970s or early 1980s have allowed a wide array of Chinese products to enter their markets duty free under their generalized system of preferences (GSP). Despite requests by China since 1979 to be granted this status, China is not a beneficiary country in the American market. Under provisions of Title V of the United States Trade Act of 1974, GSP status cannot be granted to a developing country until the country is a signatory to the GATT.

Partly as a result of these frictions in the bilateral trade relationship, China's trade with the countries of the European Economic Community (EEC) in recent years has been growing more rapidly than trade with the United States. As a result of that trend, in 1985 bilateral EEC-China trade surpassed U.S.-China trade for the first time. That margin widened in 1986: as Sino-U.S. trade fell 17 percent, Sino-EEC trade rose almost 8 percent.

Access to U.S. Credit

Not only have U.S. export controls, import restrictions and tariff policies inhibited the growth of bilateral U.S.-China trade relations, the U.S. economic relationship with China does not reflect the growing complexity evident in the case of Japan. The United States has not become a significant supplier of aid to the Chinese. Technical assistance can be provided by U.S. government agencies but only on a fee-for-service basis that in principle covers the costs incurred by the United States. Most of the official prohibitions on U.S. government credits to China were lifted, either when MFN status was granted or through subsequent legislative action. However, there is no official bilateral aid program for China administered by the United States Agency for International Development, and to date China's utilization of credits available through other channels has been modest. United States Eximbank credits of 125.5 million U.S. dollars were authorized in 1981, but no new credits were extended in the following five years. In mid-1986 new credits of 65.4 million U.S. dollars were extended to the Bank of China to finance the purchase of turbine generators, boilers and other equipment for four coal-fired electric power plants, but the magnitude of U.S. Eximbank loans continues to pale compared with those offered by the Japanese Export-Import Bank.

Second, legal challenges have kept the Chinese out of U.S. financial markets. In 1979 a suit was filed in a U.S. district court demanding payment from the Chinese government for principle and interest on Huguang railroad bonds issued by China during the Qing dynasty and sold in the United States. In 1981 a federal district judge entered a 41.3 million U.S. dollar default judgment for the bondholders. The Chinese government refused to make payments on those bonds and argued in a legal appeal that they were not responsible for the debt obligations issued by the Qing dynasty government. In 1984 the default judgment was dismissed, and in 1986 the claimants' subsequent appeal to the Circuit Court of Appeals was also dismissed. But the possibility of further legal claims may continue to keep the Chinese out of the American bond market.

Even if all legal obstacles could be overcome, there is no assurance that the Chinese would be able to sell debt obligations in the United States. Before bonds can be sold in the U.S. market they must be evaluated by U.S. rating agencies and registered with the Securities and Exchange Commission. The rating process in the United States is complex, particularly if it cannot be established legally that bonds issued by provincial or other subnational authorities constitute an engagement of the full faith and credit of the national government.

Finally, there have been only extremely modest commercial credits extended by U.S. banks. In 1985, for example, U.S. lending was only

24 million U.S. dollars, less than 10 percent of China's borrowing. Although additional credits would be readily provided by American banks, China has preferred to rely primarily on the subsidized credits provided by the World Bank and other multilateral lending agencies; the subsidized credits provided by the Japanese Overseas Economic Cooperation Fund and the Japanese Export-Import Bank; and subsidized credit provided by several countries of Western Europe. U.S. policy in recent years has been to reduce substantially the interest rate subsidies provided in Export-Import Bank loans and to work to get other developed-country Export-Import Banks to also reduce or eliminate subsidies. But other countries have failed to follow the U.S. lead with the result that the U.S. Export-Import Bank has become increasingly irrelevant.

Indeed, the only area in which the United States would appear to be ahead of the Japanese is direct investment. As discussed above, Japanese firms have established very few joint ventures in China. Moreover, Japanese participation in the search for offshore oil has been modest compared with the U.S. multinational companies. The Japanese China Oil Development Corporation, a Japanese consortium owned by the government-controlled Japan National Oil Corporation and private firms, has invested more than 600 million U.S. dollars in exploring and developing the Chengbei oil field and two other leasing sites, also in the Bohai Bay. American multinational oil exploration costs are several times higher, and U.S. firms have also invested several times more than the Japanese in joint ventures, primarily hotel and manufacturing projects.

VI. Trade with Taiwan and South Korea

Bilateral trade between China and Taiwan has grown rapidly over the past decade, but the absence of official sanction of this trade by the Taiwan authorities has meant that the volume of bilateral trade has been held far below its economic potential. Moreover, trade patterns have been somewhat unstable for reasons discussed below.

Traditionally Taiwan-China economic exchange was limited to the Taiwan purchase of medicinal herbs and special varieties of tea that were not produced domestically and were not available from other countries. People's Republic of China purchases of Taiwan goods were nominal until 1979 when Hong Kong's re-export of Taiwan goods to the People's Republic of China, notably manufactures such as synthetic fibers, building materials, cement and steel products and consumer durables such as electric fans, stereo cassette recorders and bicycles, began to escalate rapidly. By 1980 the traditional surplus of the People's Republic of China in trade with Taiwan had become deficit. As shown in Table 2, total bilateral trade jumped tenfold, from 50 million U.S. dollars in 1978 to almost half a billion U.S. dollars in 1981. Trade volume dropped in 1982 and 1983 because of a sharp fall-off in Chinese purchases of Taiwan goods, part of a larger effort to reduce the trade deficit that had emerged on the mainland in 1981. Trade recovered rapidly in 1984 and 1985 as the re-export of Taiwan goods through Hong Kong rose 170 and 230 percent, respectively. In this second phase of rapid growth China's purchases were concentrated on textile machinery, sewing machines, packaging machines, computers and accessories, color television sets and air conditioners. Two-way trade exceeded one billion U.S. dollars in 1985. As a result of this dramatic growth Taiwan is in a position of growing dependence on the China market.

Chinese-Taiwan trade, however, continues to be held far below its economic potential because of constraints imposed by the Taiwan government. The strict prohibition on direct trade means goods must be transshipped through Hong Kong rather than directly across the Taiwan Straits, increasing costs of trade and thus naturally reducing the volume of transactions. Second, the Nationalist government not only prohibits direct trade but also forbids any direct contact, negotiation or dealing with any PRC organization or any organization established by the mainland in a third country or region such as Hong Kong. In the past, Taiwan businessmen apparently have been arrested for violating the regulation prohibiting negotiations. The absence of direct contact makes it more difficult for both sides to understand the nature of the market conditions prevailing across the ninety-mile-wide body of water separating the island from the mainland.

Finally, although the Taiwan government nominally allows indirect trade, in practice it appears only to tolerate exports to the mainland, not imports. In short, the mainland has been seen as an important new market, particularly in view of rising protectionism in the West and slowing growth of world trade. But Taiwan imports of goods from the People's Republic are limited to medicinal herbs and specialty teas not available from other countries. Thus, when bilateral trade volume grew rapidly, as in 1985, the mainland experienced a large trade deficit. In 1985, for example, mainland sources reported that exports to Taiwan were only 100 million U.S. dollars, implying a deficit of 1 billion U.S. dollars. Thus in 1986, as China cut its imports to reduce its trade deficit, bilateral trade fell especially sharply. If there were a significant volume of Chinese exports to Taiwan, the bilateral trade volume would have shrunk substantially less than it did.

Trade with South Korea has also fluctuated in part for political reasons. However, unlike the case of Taiwan, the absence of a direct trade relationship has not prevented South Korean firms from seeking to establish long-range investments and a variety of forms of technical cooperation with China. Indirect trade began in the late 1970s, rising to about 400 million U.S. dollars by 1981. But in 1982, amidst extensive press reports on the flourishing bilateral economic relationship, Pyongyang protested to China over the emerging trade relationship; China substantially curtailed imports that year and in 1983. Nonetheless, the volume of bilateral trade, much of which flows directly between ports in northeastern China and South Korean ports, grew fivefold between 1983 and 1985. China's exports consist of raw materials such as wool and textile fibers as well as yarn and finished textiles. South Korean sales to China include yarn and fabrics, electrical machinery and consumer electronics such as color televisions and radios.

The bilateral economic relationship goes beyond trade. South Korean businessmen, including high-ranking executives from all of South Korea's major trading companies, have been traveling via Hong Kong to China in large numbers in recent years to explore a wide range of other potential business relations. South Korean firms are exploring technical link-ups and other forms of cooperation in the belief that the Korean level of technology is more appropriate for China than that which could be supplied by the United States, Japan or other advanced industrial states in the West. Korean construction companies are also anxious to establish cooperative relations with China. The Koreans have accumulated substantial experience in building major infrastructure projects in the Middle East and elsewhere. According to some reports a few South Korean firms have already contracted for and utilized Chinese labor in some of these projects. This is consistent with China's own drive to expand its foreign exchange earnings through international construction projects.

To facilitate the development of these cooperative relations the South Korean government in 1985 appointed a new consul general in Hong Kong, for the first time with the rank of ambassador. In the absence of official bilateral relations this envoy has become the central South Korean in the unofficial bilateral relationship.

The first South Korean-Chinese joint venture was established in 1985. The South Korean participant is the Daewoo Group, one of the country's largest industrial conglomerates, but its ownership is at least partially concealed through an elaborate ownership structure involving a U.S. subsidiary and a partially owned Hong Kong firm. The joint venture plant, a radio factory in Fujian province, will assemble color televisions and refrigerators using parts and components supplied by Daewoo.

VII. The Outlook for China's Trade

If China's foreign trade continues to grow at the pace reflected in Figure 1, it will emerge as a major international trading country by the turn of the century. Previous estimates by Western scholars have suggested that China's foreign trade might reach as much as 200 billion U.S. dollars in the year 2000, roughly the present level of foreign trade of the United Kingdom or France. Because that development would have major implications for the countries of Northeast Asia it is critical to examine the plausibility of these estimates. This examination includes an analysis of the pattern of trade growth in recent years as well as selected aspects of China's trade policies, notably the foreign trade system and exchange rate policy. These topics, an understanding of which is central to understanding China's future economic relationships in Northeast Asia, are discussed below.

The estimate that China's trade turnover in the next decade or so might reach 200 billion U.S. dollars is based more or less on straightline extrapolation at rates of growth of from 9 to 10 percent per year. Although this is well below the pace of trade expansion in the first few years of China's open-door trade policy it is well above China's longer-term historic rate of trade growth and very substantially above the rate of expansion of world trade in the 1980s. Even assuming that China's current international economic policies continue on balance to be favorable to China's increasing integration into the world economy, what is the prospect for sustaining China's trade growth?

In the short run, say to 1990, there are several reasons to doubt that China's trade can continue to grow as rapidly as in the recent past. The relevant factors include trends in international product markets and China's need to adjust to the record trade deficits of 1985 and 1986.

The most salient international factors include the collapse of international prices for oil and petroleum products and the increased restrictions imposed by Western industrialized countries on the sale of Chinese textile products.

The Effect of Lower Petroleum Prices

China is particularly vulnerable to the 1985-1986 collapse in oil prices since petroleum and related products are among China's most important export products and have grown rapidly in recent years. Chinese oil exports began on a very modest scale in the 1960s and did not surpass a million metric tons annually until 1973. They passed ten million metric tons in 1978 and were on a plateau of thirteen to fifteen million metric tons in 1979-1983. But in 1984 and 1985 exports grew rapidly to twenty-two and thirty million metric tons, respectively. Thus 1985 exports, the equivalent of six hundred thousand barrels per day, were roughly half those of Nigeria and Libya and placed China among the top dozen petroleum exporters in the world. Earnings from petroleum exports in 1985, which included about six million metric tons of refined products in addition to thirty million metric tons of crude, were well over 6 billion U.S. dollars, fully one-fourth of China's total export earnings. The sharp decline in the price of crude beginning in late 1985 and continuing in most of 1986, combined with a modest reduction in the volume of oil exports, discussed further below, reduced China's export earnings in 1986 by about 3 billion U.S. dollars or 10 percent. Coal has been subject to a similar negative price trend in international markets, but China's loss of foreign exchange earnings from coal exports was much smaller since the value of exports in 1986 of 9.6 million tons was substantially less than that for petroleum and related products.

There is little possibility that China could increase its petroleum export volume to compensate for the decline in the world market price. Most importantly, China's current level of exports has seriously exacerbated its domestic energy shortages. Exports could be increased, but only at a significant cost in terms of additional closures of factories and losses of domestic industrial output.

Second, and especially significant, China's petroleum exports by 1985 had become so large that they probably began to have a perceptible effect on the world market price. In 1978, exports were only two hundred thousand barrels a day and as many as eighteen or nineteen countries were more important than China as world suppliers. But by 1985 China's oil export volume had tripled and its rank among world petroleum exporters had increased to twelfth. In recognition of the relationship between the magnitude of its own exports and the world price, China announced in April 1986 that its export volume would be held at the same level as 1985. Later in the year, as the price of oil continued to slip, the Chinese announced in September that the volume of exports had actually been cut and in the second half of the year would be cut by an additional forty thousand barrels per day in order to support the mid-1986 OPEC agreement to curtail production to increase the world price.

China's Trade Deficits, 1984-1986

On the domestic side we must recognize that the rapid trade growth in recent years has been characterized by an increasing trade deficit.

The trade deficit in 1984 was a modest 1.3 billion U.S. dollars but skyrocketed to 14.9 billion U.S. dollars in 1985. That deficit, equal to more than half of export earnings, was financed by sharply drawing down China's foreign exchange reserves, by stepping up international borrowing and through the foreign exchange acquired by direct foreign investment in China. Holdings of foreign exchange dropped from 16.7 billion U.S. dollars to 11.9 billion U.S. dollars during the year, a fall of almost a third. According to IMF estimates, borrowing in various forms increased by almost 8 billion U.S. dollars to total about 20 billion U.S. dollars. The surge of borrowing, particularly by China's enterprises borrowing independently from the Bank of China, was so great that the official data fell 4 billion U.S. dollars short of the total borrowing reported in foreign sources.

Despite remedial measures, described below, China's huge foreign trade deficit continued in 1986. Although exports rose modestly while imports dropped slightly, the deficit in 1986 was estimated at about 11 billion U.S. dollars, second only to the record deficit of 1985. China's foreign exchange reserves fell even further in 1986, dropping to just over 10 billion U.S. dollars by the end of the third quarter. But that further draw down of reserves financed only a small part of the total deficit since reserves had already been reduced to the equivalent of only a few months of import purchases.

The Chinese took three additional steps to finance the deficit in 1986. First, China negotiated its first stand-by credit, for 712 million U.S. dollars, from the International Monetary Fund. The credit was requested as part of a 1986-1987 economic adjustment program designed to reduce the trade deficit by 1987 to an amount sufficiently small to be covered by concessional loans at reduced interest rates, thus eliminating the need for further borrowing from commercial banks. The credit line, which was extended conditional upon the deficit reduction program, carries a 6 percent interest charge and is to be repaid over five years.

Second, the Chinese appear to have sold 1 billion U.S. dollars in nonmonetary gold in the first ten months of 1986. China is among the top ten producers of gold in the world, and domestic production has been increasing at double-digit rates in recent years in response to the much higher prices offered for sale of the metal to the government. In the second quarter the Chinese sold 0.5 billion dollars of gold on the London market to gain foreign exchange to finance a portion of the continuing current account deficit. Additional sales occurred in July and October, and when monthly trade data for November and December are published total gold sales might exceed 1.5 billion U.S. dollars.

Third and finally, China's foreign debt jumped by another 7 billion

U.S. dollars to reach an estimated 27 billion U.S. dollars at the end of 1986.

On the presumption that China's application to the IMF for stand-by credit is an accurate reflection of China's intention of no new foreign bank borrowing after 1987, China must dramatically increase its sales of products in international markets if it is to avoid the unpleasant alternative of scaling back imports, a process begun on a very modest scale in 1986. Yet this is precisely what China has failed to do in the recent past, despite several policy initiatives designed to promote exports. This problem is reflected in Figure 1, which shows that Chinese exports grew only 5 billion U.S. dollars or less than one-quarter between 1981 and 1985. During the same period imports grew more than 20 billion U.S. dollars, more than 90 percent. Of the increase in exports during this period fully 3 billion U.S. dollars or 60 percent of the total growth came from the increased sale of petroleum and refined petroleum products. China was much less successful in increasing its sales of manufactured goods. Even in 1986 in the wake of an unprecedented current account deficit the rise in exports was modest, particularly if we take into account the half-billion U.S. dollar sale of gold.

China's Energy Exports

Increased dependence on the sale of raw materials, energy and other primary products is problematic for several reasons. First, the volatility of raw material and energy product prices in international markets makes China more vulnerable to export earnings fluctuations, as was particularly evident when crude oil prices fell in 1986.

Second, and far more significant, there is considerable reason to believe that China should not be an energy exporter at all and that economic growth would be more rapid if the energy sold abroad were used at home. China's industry has been handicapped, for more than a decade, by critical energy shortages. In many cities industrial plants are closed down several days a week because of insufficient electric power. The gap between demand and supply of electricity for industry is estimated at about fifty billion kilowatt hours annually, causing industry to operate at least 25 percent below capacity in recent years.

More recently, energy shortages have become acute in agriculture as well. As China's agricultural sector has modernized and peasants have experienced rising levels of real income in the last decade, the amount of farm machinery has risen considerably. In 1984 there were well over four million farm tractors. But available supplies of gasoline and diesel fuel limited the average use of each tractor to only two hundred hours annually or about a half-hour per day. Peasants in many areas where fuel was unavailable through normal channels stopped fuel distribution trucks on the roads and forced the drivers to make sales on the spot.

The shortfall of energy supplies first became acute when, in the late 1970s, after a decade of extremely rapid growth, oil production levelled off at something barely over one hundred million metric tons annually (two million barrels a day), while industrial production continued to grow relatively rapidly. While production of energy sources began to rise again, coal starting in 1982 and petroleum in 1984, the energy crunch inexplicably worsened. What was not immediately recognized was that as China's oil production went from 106 million metric tons in 1983 to 125 million metric tons in 1985, more than 80 percent of the incremental output was sold on international markets either as crude petroleum or as refined products. Why, in the face of an acute domestic energy shortage, did China sell a huge share of its growing oil output on the international market? Several causes are evident, although it is difficult for an outside observer to be very confident in weighing the relative importance of each.

Perhaps most important, China's entire foreign trade system has been and continues to be under intense pressure to accelerate exports to pay for a growing volume of imports that are thought necessary to achieve the ambitious development goals set for the Sixth (1981-1985) and Seventh (1986-1990) Five-Year Plans and for the longer-term year 2000 goals. In the short term it was easier to sell increased quantities of a homogeneous product, crude oil, into a well-established world energy market than it was to develop new markets for manufactured goods, particularly since the quality of many of China's manufactures is well below international standards.

Moreover, peculiarities of China's internal price structure provide substantial incentives to sell crude oil in the international rather than the domestic market. Crude oil, like many other raw materials, is substantially underpriced on the domestic market. For example, its price in 1985 was about one-seventh to one-eighth of the international price. But the China National Chemical Import and Export Corporation (also known as Sinochem), the foreign trade corporation with the sole authority to buy and sell petroleum products in the international market, had a substantial incentive to sell crude internationally. The corporation could purchase oil from the wells of the domestic industry, under the Ministry of Petroleum, at the low domestic price and then turn around and sell the product in the international market. Since the domestic price was set artificially low, these transactions generated enormous profits for the foreign trade corporation handling the transactions. Indeed, these high profits were widely trumpeted in China's domestic press in 1986 when Sinochem was held up as China's single most profitable foreign trade corporation in 1985. The real economic value of these profits, however, was challenged by domestic manufacturing firms that had been idle for much of the year. The real value of what they could have produced with the same energy might have been greater than the earnings from the sale of the energy in the international market.

Finally, past mistakes in domestic allocation of investment resources probably contributed to the tendency to sell the oil on the international rather than the domestic market. First, China in recent years has probably underinvested in refining capacity so that in 1983-1985 refining capacity fell behind production. If crude could not be refined for domestic use perhaps exports were rational after all. But this is not a fully convincing argument since much of China's crude oil is not refined but burned as bunker to generate electricity. About one-fourth of all electric power produced in thermal power stations depends on oil for fuel. China has also underinvested in its domestic distribution system. The rail, pipeline and truck distribution systems for crude and refined products are woefully inadequate. As pointed out above, in the early 1980s decisions were made to increase the capacity of pipelines and other distribution systems to take China's crude to ports for export. Comparable investments to distribute energy to domestic producers have lagged. Thus in the short run, as production of crude oil rose the incremental output may have been easier to sell on the international than the domestic market.

Direct Foreign Investment

Foreign investment in China is sometimes seen as a solution to the dilemma discussed above. If exports cannot pay for the Western machinery, equipment and technology that the Chinese feel is necessary to sustain their modernization, perhaps foreigners will supply the necessary goods in joint ventures and other forms of cooperation that do not require Chinese expenditure of foreign exchange. In short, it may be in some cases easier to finance an excess of imports over exports via foreign direct investment than foreign borrowing.

The Chinese publish numerous, seemingly inconsistent data on direct foreign investment flows, which makes empirical analysis particularly uncertain. For example, although they sometimes utilize the same accounting categories for recording foreign investment in China, the data published by the Ministry of Foreign Economic Relations and Trade (MOFERT) differ from those compiled and released by other state agencies, both in the total reported amount of direct foreign investment and in the specific subitems. Of the several sources, the MOFERT data are probably the more reliable and are incorporated in Figure 2.

Total direct foreign investment in China, inclusive of foreign funds committed in equity joint ventures, contractual joint ventures, cooperative resource exploitation (almost entirely in oil exploration and development contracts), wholly foreign owned firms and compensation trade, showed a strong upward trend through 1985. During the first four years (1979-1982) in which China actively sought foreign investment, the amount of capital actually utilized (as distinguished from reported contracted amounts which, for a variety of reasons, frequently fail to materialize) averaged only 440 million U.S. dollars. In 1983, 1984 and 1985 these capital flows rose regularly from .92 to 1.42 and then to 1.96 billion U.S. dollars, respectively.

While some Chinese have been disappointed that they have not been able to attract more foreign investment, the inflow of almost 2 billion U.S. dollars by 1985 was a rather substantial achievement. Direct foreign investment in China that year was several times the level of direct foreign investment in either Taiwan or South Korea and appears to have been greater than that in any other developing country.

While China had achieved significant early success in attracting foreign investment, the data for 1986, as indicated in Figure 2, show a sharp decline in the rate of growth of foreign investment. Even more striking, the volume of foreign investment contracts signed in 1986, an important indication of the future flow of capital, declined by fifty percent. The causes of that precipitous decline are numerous and well known. First among them is the requirement that each joint venture project be self-sufficient in terms of foreign exchange. In short it is nearly impossible to convert local currerčy earnings into foreign exchange. What that means is that even a project that provides a product that was formerly imported, and thus saves large amounts of foreign exchange, must earn convertible currency from the international sale of its products in order to provide foreign exchange for the foreign partner. The government will not provide foreign funds in exchange for products sold on the domestic markets, even when they reap foreign exchange savings. The result is that once the few joint venture projects with high export potential were launched it became more difficult to sustain the flow of direct investment funds, and the value of contracts signed began to fall sharply.

Beyond that fundamental problem, foreign firms have found it far more difficult and costly to operate in China than they originaly anticipated. The costs of maintaining offices have risen so greatly that they now exceed costs in Hong Kong. Labor costs for manufacturing firms have been inflated by the government to the point that they now

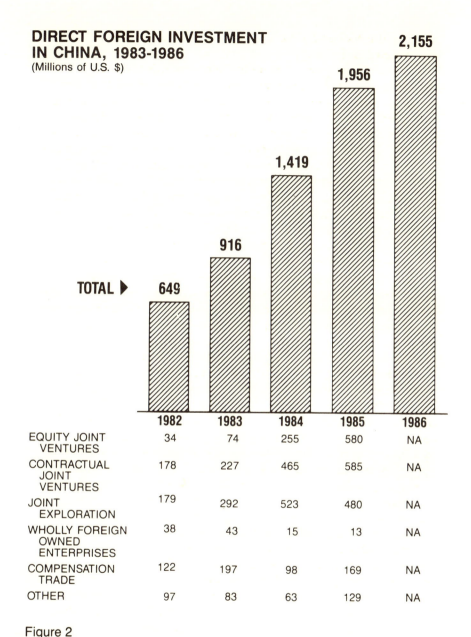

DIRECT FOREIGN INVESTMENT IN CHINA, 1983-1986
(Millions of U.S. $)

	1982	1983	1984	1985	1986
TOTAL ▶	649	916	1,419	1,956	2,155
EQUITY JOINT VENTURES	34	74	255	580	NA
CONTRACTUAL JOINT VENTURES	178	227	465	585	NA
JOINT EXPLORATION	179	292	523	480	NA
WHOLLY FOREIGN OWNED ENTERPRISES	38	43	15	13	NA
COMPENSATION TRADE	122	197	98	169	NA
OTHER	97	83	63	129	NA

Figure 2

Sources: Ministry of Foreign Economic Relations and Trade, *Almanac of China's Foreign Economic Relations and Trade 1984*, p.1095; *Almanac of China's Foreign Economic Relations and Trade 1985*, p.1066; *Almanac of China's Foreign Economic Relations and Trade 1986*, p.1212; and *People's Daily*, January 24, 1987, p.1.

exceed some other Asian countries, fundamentally undermining what should be China's main attraction to foreign investors, low cost labor. As a result, the only large joint ventures in which there was any progress in 1986 were those tied to the exploitation of natural resources, notably coal.

Summary

While China's foreign trade growth for the first decade of its open policy was spectacular, it seems unlikely that this pace can be sustained. Rapid growth of imports, particularly in 1984 and 1985, was made possible by the sale of petroleum, which entailed a significant cost in terms of slower domestic growth; the draw down of billions of dollars in previously accumulated foreign exchange reserves, that by the end of 1986 were virtually depleted; and the accumulation of foreign debt estimated by the IMF to stand at more than 27 billion U.S. dollars at the end of 1986. Moreover, foreign investment, which by 1985 financed a significant share of the current account deficit, grew significantly more slowly in 1986 compared to previous years and probably will fall in 1987.

Although further liberalization of the terms under which foreigners could operate in China might sustain the growth of direct foreign investment, it is not clear whether it is politically feasible to adopt the concessions that would be necessary to stimulate increased foreign interest in investing in China. Moreover, even should this occur it is important to keep the likely magnitude of foreign investment in mind. China's import bill is currently running at more than 40 billion U.S. dollars per year. Even should the growth of direct investment resume the upward course that was interrupted in 1986, it is extremely unlikely that direct foreign investment would ever pay for more than a very small share of China's imports. While that investment may be critically important for technology transfer in selected industries, China must increase its exports significantly if import growth is to be maintained. And, as will be shown in the next section, export growth depends over the longer term on further economic reform in China.

VIII. A Longer-Term Perspective

Over the longer run China's increased integration in the world economy will to a large degree depend on the extent to which it moves away from its traditional import substitution strategy toward a policy of export promotion. The former takes as its basic long-term objective the creation of the capability to produce domestically most if not all of the manufactured goods initially acquired on international markets. That objective is achieved through high import tariffs, which protect domestic industries against foreign competition; through an overvalued exchange rate, which is thought necessary to reduce the domestic cost of acquiring capital goods and necessary intermediate inputs from the international market but which inevitably also undermines the incentives for domestic firms to sell on the international market; and import licensing and foreign exchange controls, frequently including multiple exchange rates, which attempt to mitigate the effects of the overvaluation of the domestic currency in the foreign exchange market. The best contemporary exemplars of this approach to development are countries in Latin America where tariff protection of domestic industries that began under the guise of supporting infant manufacturing industries that would ultimately become competitive in international markets frequently has led to increased inefficiency in production and a long-term inability to compete internationally except with enormous subsidies. The contrary pattern of export promotion is more characteristic of the rapidly modernizing countries of East Asia, notably Taiwan after about 1960, South Korea and of course Hong Kong.

In many respects China's economic policies in recent years have moved away from import substitution toward export promotion. These include reforms of the foreign trade bureaucracy and a substantial devaluation of the Chinese currency, the yuan.

The Foreign Trade System

In the early 1950s the Chinese borrowed the Soviet-style foreign trade system. The key feature, of course, was that foreign trade became a monopoly of the state carried out by foreign trade corporations organized under the direction of the Ministry of Foreign Trade. The corporations were organized along product lines parallel to the industrial production ministries. They also were vertically organized with head offices in Beijing and branches in most of the provincial capitals. The key economic feature of the system was the complete insulation of domestic firms from the international market.

Domestic firms could not sell directly on the international market, nor were they subject to competition from foreign firms. The system of foreign trade corporations also worked in reverse to frustrate the access of foreign firms to the domestic Chinese market. Rather than being able to sell their products directly to factories that would utilize the goods, the "end-users," foreigners were forced to work through the foreign trade corporations. In 1979 China's foreign trade was almost entirely under the direct control of ten national import and export corporations under the Ministry of Foreign Trade.

Beginning in the early 1980s this centralized, vertically controlled system began to erode as individual provinces, major municipalities and industrial ministries were able to set up their own trading entities, undermining the monopoly power of the Ministry of Foreign Trade for many product lines. By the mid-1980s literally hundreds of these new corporations were regularly entering into export and import transactions, and the number of trading corporations was expected to expand to about one thousand.

Simultaneously, the number of export and import commodities that were under the exclusive control of the ministry's trade corporations shrank considerably. By the mid-1980s they reportedly had the exclusive control of only seven import commodities: steel, fertilizer, rubber, timber, tobacco, polyester fiber and grain; and sixteen export commodities: rice, soybeans, peanuts, frozen pork, cotton, cotton yarn, cotton grey goods, drawn work, tea, tobacco, crude oil, refined petroleum products and coal. All other commodities could be bought or sold by the roughly six hundred trading corporations organized by the various industrial ministries, provinces and major municipalities.

Second, there were sweeping changes in the control of foreign exchange. Under the traditional system the foreign exchange proceeds from exports were retained entirely within the foreign trade corporation system. Earnings from international sales were used to finance imports via a system of implicit foreign exchange rationing. Domestic producers of export goods did not gain any foreign exchange or any explicit right to use foreign exchange to purchase imports. Access to imported goods was controlled bureaucratically, and users did not have to pay for imports with foreign exchange. This insulation between the domestic and foreign markets has led some foreign observers to characterize the foreign trade corporations as establishing an airlock between domestic and foreign markets.

When the reforms were introduced, firms selling goods in the international market were allowed to retain a fixed share of their export earnings in foreign exchange, thus establishing an explicit potential command over foreign goods. Under the present system only three-quarters of the foreign exchange earnings are controlled by the foreign trade corporations. The remaining one-fourth is divided between the enterprise and the local government. Thus for the first time firms have a direct incentive to sell on the international market.

Exchange Rate Policy

Like other centrally planned economies, China adopted an administratively set foreign exchange rate and the Bank of China assumed complete control of the country's foreign exchange transactions. The actual exchange rate was not very important since after China's entry into the Korean War in 1950 the United States and other·Western industrialized countries imposed an embargo on trade with China and thus the great bulk of China's trade was carried out on a bilateral barter basis with other centrally planned economies.

By the 1960s, after the break with Moscow, trade with market-oriented economies increased significantly, but since all trade was under the monopoly control of the foreign trade corporations of the Ministry of Foreign Trade, the exchange rate was not a major determinant of trade decisions. Domestic producers of export goods sold them to the appropriate foreign trade corporation at the same price as goods sold in the domestic market so these firms were not affected by either the level of or changes in the exchange rate. Similarly, imported goods prices in the domestic market were not affected by the exchange rate since the foreign trade corporations followed a practice of setting the price of imports at the same level as comparable domestically produced goods. Thus changes in the exchange rate could not affect the prices of exports and imports and would have no direct effect on the volume of imports and exports. Imports were determined by shortfalls between planned needs and planned domestic output and exports were regarded primarily as a means to finance this planned level of imports.

After foreign trade decision-making began to be decentralized in the late 1970s, the exchange rate between the Chinese yuan and foreign currencies began to play a significant role in foreign trade decisions. As reflected in Figure 3, since that time the Bank of China has systematically devalued the yuan vis-à-vis the U.S. dollar. By mid-1986 the value of the yuan was less than half the level of 1979. Most of the drop occurred in 1985 and 1986, a period when the value of the dollar against many other currencies was also falling substantially. Thus the yuan has fallen even more against the Japanese yen, the Deutschmark and currencies of other major industrial countries.

When the reform of China's foreign trade system began in the late 1970s the exchange rate was 1.55 yuan to the U.S. dollar. In 1979 and 1980, as the exchange rate remained almost constant, China's imports began to run significantly ahead of exports, and a number of steps were taken in an attempt to alleviate the trade deficit. Among the most significant changes was the introduction in 1981 of an internal settlement rate, a new exchange rate offered by the Bank of China to Chinese trading organizations, which effectively substantially devalued the Chinese domestic currency. Immediately prior to the introduction of the internal rate, firms that sold products on the international market received only 1.5 units of domestic currency for each U.S. dollar's worth of international sales. With the new internal rate they were credited with 2.8 yuan or 87 percent more units of domestic currency than previously. The internal settlement system was thus designed to provide substantially greater incentives for Chinese firms to export. But the official rate, which fell in value much more slowly, also was maintained so that foreign tourists travelling in China or Chinese citizens cashing in remittances received from their relatives abroad did not receive the benefit of the devaluation of the domestic currency. Similarly, the internal settlement rate made imported goods more expensive in China since importers beginning in 1981 had to pay the Bank of China 2.8 units of domestic currency for each U.S. dollar's worth of imports. Obviously, in theory, the net effect of the internal settlement rate should have been to increase the volume of exports relative to the volume of imports.

In practice it appears that the demand for imported goods was rather price inelastic. If potential importers had the authority to act on their own or they could get approval to bring products into China, in many cases they were prepared to pay seemingly unlimited amounts of domestic currency to buy a dollar's worth of imports. In part that reflected the easy access to domestic credit—the so-called soft budget constraint. Many firms could borrow almost unlimited amounts of domestic currency from the People's Bank and use the proceeds to purchase dollars from the Bank of China. Since most firms were able to pass along the costs of borrowing or were in no way penalized if higher interest payments cut into their profits, the demand for foreign exchange was not effectively curtailed by the higher internal settlement rate. Thus, traditional bureaucratic mechanisms were used to control the trade deficit, and in 1982 and 1983 a trade surplus was re-established.

But in 1984 and 1985, when trade controls were relaxed somewhat, an even larger deficit emerged. This time, unlike 1979 and 1981, as the deficit emerged in 1984 and expanded in 1985 the value of the domestic currency was steadily devalued. In early 1985 the rate stood at 2.8 yuan to the U.S. dollar.

In the first months of 1986 the deficit continued at a seemingly unabated pace. A further sharp devaluation took place in early July when the Bank of China lowered the value of the domestic currency

THE VALUE OF THE CHINESE YUAN

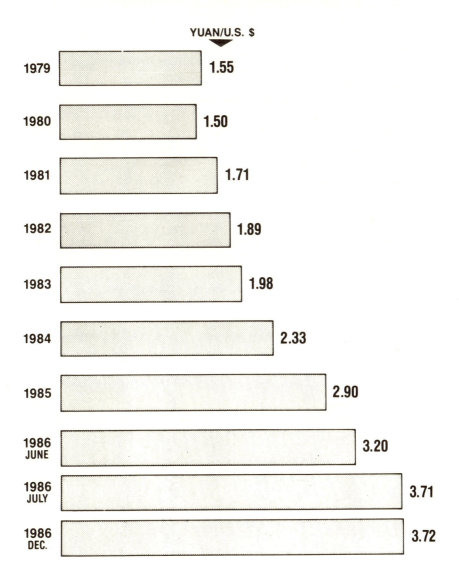

Figure 3

Source: Bank of China.

by about 15.8 percent. By mid-1986 the exchange rate stood at 3.70, and the value of the yuan in terms of the U.S. dollar was then about 40 percent of what it had been in 1980. Despite this drastic devaluation, administrative means, such as a prohibition on the further import of automobiles and certain types of consumer durables, are still critical to efforts to reduce the trade deficit.

Because the official exchange rate surpassed the internal settlement rate of 2.8 in early 1985, the World Bank and others reported that the internal settlement rate system had been formally or at least de facto abolished. If exporters could earn more than 3.0 yuan per U.S. dollar in the official market by early 1986, why would they wish to sell their dollars at 2.8 yuan on the internal market? However, the Bank of China has never formally announced the abolition of the internal settlement system, and I believe that an internal rate above the official rate continues to be used in many trade transactions.

In addition to devaluing substantially the value of the domestic currency, the Chinese have reduced the number of commodities subject to export taxes. For most goods that are sold at established international prices in competitive markets exporters are unable to pass along the cost of the export tariff to international buyers—those buyers would be able to purchase the goods more cheaply from other sources if they were faced with the international price plus the export tariff. In fully competitive markets the producer would have to lower the price of its goods by the full amount of the export tax. Thus the export tariff cuts into the earnings of the exporter and reduces the incentive to try to sell on the world market. In the spring of 1986 the Chinese reduced the number of commodities subject to export tariffs in an attempt to stimulate world market sales. The process continued in 1987 with the elimination of the export tariff on coal.

Comparative Advantage Trade versus Continued Self-Reliance

While China has reorganized its foreign trade apparatus, undertaken substantial changes in its exchange rate system and curtailed export taxes on some goods in order to promote the growth of exports, the transition from import substitution to export promotion is still very partial. Although China's highest political leaders frequently reiterate their support of what has come to be called the "open door policy," they have not necessarily fully understood the necessity of transforming their attitude toward international trade. That attitude is perhaps reflected in Premier Zhao Ziyang's report to China's National People's Congress, in the spring of 1986, on the Seventh Five-Year Plan (1986-1990). On international economic issues he began by recounting the successes achieved under the open door policy and spoke of the need to become more competitive in international markets. But, strikingly, he also called for China to "make every effort to produce at home whatever we can" and "to expand production of import substitutes and to increase the proportion of goods produced at home," words that could well have been spoken by Mao Zedong in the period of most extreme autarky and self-reliance. Perhaps the emphasis on import substitution and self-reliance does not reflect the true thinking of China's reformist leadership but is intended for those elements within the Chinese leadership who oppose China's opening policy. But whether these formulations represent a dominant or minority view, they are troubling since they leave no room for the pursuit of a long-term trade strategy based on China's underlying comparative advantage.

Similarly, there is a seeming reluctance on the part of the Bank of China to commit to eventual convertibility of the yuan, which is almost certainly a prerequisite to China's long-term integration into the world economy. In certain respects there is an implicit recognition that convertibility is, in the long-term, desirable. When the internal settlement rate was introduced in 1981 the Chinese went to great pains to deny that the new system effectively had introduced a multiple exchange rate system, generally regarded as a step away from convertibility and inconsistent with the charter of the General Agreement on Tariffs and Trade. But when asked, Chinese officials in the Ministry of Foreign Economic Relations and Trade deny that the post-1980 devaluations of the domestic currency represent an attempt to move toward a freely convertible yuan.

The Relation between Urban Reform and Trade Growth

Over the long run the pace of integration of China in the world economy will also depend on the degree of success of China's urban, industrial economic reforms. The reasons for this relationship are several. First, and most obvious, successful economic reform is likely to lead to more rapid development of the Chinese economy that, other things being equal, will increase the supply of goods for export and increase the internal demand for imports. Second, and probably more important, successful domestic reform would imply that domestic firms had increased substantially their ability to adapt to changing market conditions, to raise product quality, and to control costs—all developments that would increase substantially China's ability to sell manufactured goods on the world market.

How important could this be to increased trade? The lessons of China's agriculture, where reforms began sooner and have clearly been more successful, give some indication. This is not the place to discuss the origins and policies of agricultural reform. But the spectacular results can be easily conveyed. Between 1978 and 1985, in response to a series of reforms begun in 1976 and 1977, Chinese cereal output grew by a hundred million metric tons, as much as in the previous twenty years. But the pace of increased production was even more rapid for a broad range of nongrain crops and other components of agriculture—cotton, oil-bearing seeds, meat, poultry and so forth. The rate of growth of farm output has been so rapid that it has propelled China's gross national product ahead at an above-average rate even though industrial growth in some years has been below average.

The transformation of China's agriculture from a lagging to a leading sector has had major implications for China's foreign trade. Prior to 1978, imports of foodgrain crops had been rising steadily and a significant share of the population living in China's larger cities was entirely dependent on imported cereals for their basic consumption needs. Wheat imports, which became significant in the crisis years of the early 1960s following the Great Leap Forward (1958-1960), averaged eight million tons in 1977-1979, and passed the ten million metric ton mark in 1980. The peak level of imports came in 1982 when the total rose to almost fourteen million metric tons, making China one of the world's largest wheat importers. By 1985, in response to sharply higher domestic prices and increased incentives for domestic marketing by farmers, wheat output had increased by about thirty million tons compared to 1978 and wheat imports fell to a twenty-five year low of 840,000 tons. Moreover, exports of other grains, notably corn, grew so rapidly that despite a slight drop in domestic grain production in 1985 China became a net exporter of cereals for the first time since 1960. Corn exports, largely to South Korea, Japan and the Soviet Union, rose to 6.2 million metric tons in 1985. China also established new agricultural markets in Southeast Asia, selling one hundred fifty thousand tons of soybeans to Indonesia replacing the United States as the major supplier in that market. In the mid-1980s China was posting all-time peak levels of net exports of agricultural commodities.

The reform of the urban industrial sector is potentially more far-reaching than that in agriculture for two reasons. One, manufacturing is more important to China's economy than is agriculture. That is somewhat surprising, given that two-thirds or more of the population reside in rural areas, and the great majority of these are engaged in agricultural production. But the manufacturing sector contributes a larger share of total national output than does agriculture. That is a result of the enormous emphasis the Chinese Communist Party has always placed on industrial development. From the 1950s through the 1970s the party allocated far more resources to industrial development than to agriculture. As a result of that

46

emphasis and related policies, the long-term expansion of industry has been several times more rapid than that of farming.

Despite this rapid industrial expansion, manufacturing has lagged behind agriculture in recent years in terms of productivity, that is, the amount of output produced per unit of capital and labor used in production. In short, greater manufacturing output has been achieved primarily through massive increases in the stock of machinery and equipment utilized and a slower but still significant growth of the industrial labor force. But efficiency lagged far behind.

The goal of the urban industrial reform, which was initiated in certain cities and selected types of manufacturing in the early 1980s and adopted as a national-scale program in the fall of 1984, is to utilize the existing plant and equipment far more efficiently, to raise the growth of manufactured goods output without a proportionate increase in the required capital stock.

Not only does manufacturing contribute a larger share than agriculture to China's national income, China's true comparative advantage in the world market almost certainly lies in the area of labor-intensive manufactured goods, not the primary products, such as crude oil, and agricultural products, such as cereals, that have played such an important role in export growth in recent years. As already noted above, energy could be used to greater advantage in China's domestic industry. Given that China's endowment of arable land per capita is among the lowest in the world, it is also very improbable that China has a comparative advantage in agricultural products, except possibly very labor-intensive specialty crops such as mushrooms, mulberry leaves (for raising silk worms), tea and so forth. Increased dynamism in manufacturing will be accompanied by an ability to respond to changing world market conditions, to meet the quality and variety standards of the international marketplace and so forth.

In short, a successful urban industrial reform will both increase the underlying growth of the Chinese economy and increase its competitiveness in international markets and thus likely lead to greater integration in the world economy.

Summary

The analysis of both short-term and more systemic factors in this and the previous section lead to a relatively cautious prognosis for China's foreign trade and investment. Although Chinese trade will almost certainly grow significantly, the pace of trade expansion is likely to be well below that of recent years. Given the virtual leveling off in total trade turnover in 1986 and China's commitment to the IMF to reduce its trade deficit further in 1987, it seems likely that China will fall somewhat short of its plan to increase trade volume 50 percent in the course of the present five-year plan (1986-1990).

Even if the foreign trade plan were to be fulfilled, the economic center of gravity in Northeast Asia will very much remain Japan. For example, if China were able to achieve its 1990 trade target its trade would still be less than half of Japanese trade turnover of 1980. And despite increased trade with China, Japan is almost certain to remain the most important trading partner in the region for South Korea and Taiwan. Although China's population is much larger than Japan's, its per capita income is a tiny fraction of that of Japan, a fraction that is not likely to grow very significantly in the medium term. As a result Japan's trade is certain to remain several times that of China. Thus, while the trend of increased intraregional economic integration may be further enhanced by the expanding role of China in the region and China may rank as an important trade partner for South Korea and Taiwan, their trade relations will still remain very much centered on Japan within the region and the United States outside of the region. Mongolian and North Korean trade seem likely to remain preponderantly with the Soviet Union. Only in the cases of Hong Kong and Japan is trade with China likely to loom large.

Moreover, while there may be a further increase in the relative importance of intraregional trade, that trend is likely to reflect the sum of the individual bilateral trade relationships within the region rather than the emergence of any institutional framework that would have regional economic integration as a goal. The differences in underlying economic systems, huge disparities in the existing levels of economic development and lack of shared objectives among the nations of the region appear to preclude the development of specific arrangements leading to greater regional integration. Of the major nations, only Japan appears to have a comprehensive economic strategy toward the region, and it clearly prefers to achieve its goals on a bilateral basis. It is noteworthy that Japan is the only nation in the region that has direct trade ties with all the other nations in the region, including North Korea and Mongolia. China's own opening strategy has no clearly defined Northeast Asian component. Elements of a comprehensive Soviet economic strategy toward the region have begun to emerge, but the full dimensions remain obscure. Thus while intraregional trade may grow we are not likely to witness any time soon the development of a Northeast Asia regional economic system.

IX. Implications for U.S. Policy

China's emergence as a major economic power has important implications for the United States because of the expansion of direct bilateral economic relations, because of Sino-U.S. competition in third-country markets and because of the broader effects of a rapidly modernizing China on Northeast Asia and the world economy. Despite these multiple sources of importance of China's modernization, the United States has no consistent strategy to deal with the rise of the People's Republic of China as a major economic power. The articulated premise of our policy toward China beginning in the Carter administration was that a strong, secure and modernizing China is in our long-run interest. The United States would prefer a China that is politically stable, capable at a minimum of feeding its huge and growing population without placing extraordinary demands on world food markets, and which is drawn into world product and capital markets rather than remaining inward looking. That formulation was expressed most explicitly by Vice-President Walter Mondale in a major address in Beijing in 1979.

Yet there was a gulf between this broad vision of and support in principle for a modernizing China, on the one hand, and specific U.S. policies, on the other. As discussed above, these policies restrict Chinese access to the U.S. market, deny GSP status for Chinese goods and deny bilateral economic aid for China. This does not constitute an argument for eliminating quotas on Chinese sales of textiles, granting GSP status to China or initiating an aid program. It simply notes the disparity between the broad vision presented to justify the opening of formal diplomatic relations on the one hand and specific foreign economic policies on the other.

Security vs. Economic Cooperation

In part, the lack of a coherent economic strategy reflects a continuing U.S. preoccupation with the potential security dimension of the bilateral relationship. In short, China's importance has been defined primarily as military rather than economic. This was implicit in the initial opening of the Nixon administration to China in 1971-1972, became explicit during the Carter administration when the U.S. Secretary of Defense Harold Brown visited China in January 1980 and continues under the Reagan administration. During the Brown visit the United States announced its willingness to sell radar, transport aircraft, communications equipment and other nonlethal military equipment. Despite the lack of any military sales, under the Reagan administration the policy was expanded to include a willingness to sell certain types of arms to China. Numerous high ranking officals from both the Departments of State and Defense have reiterated the priority the United States gives to building an enduring military relationship with China to assist China in deterring the Soviet Union in East Asia.

This continuing attempt to develop a closer military relationship, reflected in repeated visits by successive U.S. defense secretaries and the early 1985 visit of the chairman of the Joint Chiefs of Staff, seems ill-advised on several grounds. Most important, a strategic relationship does not provide the soundest basis for a sustainable bilateral relationship between China and the United States. It has been clear from the outset of China's renewed modernization and reform drive in the late 1970s that military modernization is the lowest priority for the Chinese, following the modernization of agriculture, industry and science and technology. China's own defense spending has been falling, not only as a share of total government spending but even in absolute terms in recent years. Budgetary outlays in the defense category in 1984 fell to an all-time low of 11.7 percent of government spending at all levels.

Not only is military modernization a low priority, but the Chinese may be reluctant to buy significant quantities of arms because they perceive the U.S. attempt to develop a security relationship as part of a policy of continued arms sales to Taiwan. The United States sought, through a joint communique issued with China in August 1982, to establish Beijing's acquiescence of continued arms sales to Taiwan. But the Chinese government has not shared that interpretation of the communique and has objected on several occasions since the communique to continued U.S. arms sales to Taiwan. Some high-ranking officials in the Reagan administration believe that if China would make significant arms purchases from the United States it could not continue to object to continued sales by the United States of arms to Taiwan. But the Chinese are not likely to drop their objections to U.S. military sales to Taiwan and have made only very selective purchases of U.S. military equipment.

Second, China is militarily so weak that no conceivable amount of purchases of military-related technology or even of conventional arms is likely to affect the strategic balance. Thus, China's potential role in a strategic relationship directed implicitly against the Soviet Union is, in my view, largely a mirage.

The Chinese themselves seem at least as much interested in how Western military technology could be used to increase their own sales in the international arms market as in what the technology might do for their own military capabilities. A 550 million U.S. dollar purchase of avionics kits from the United States in 1986, the largest military purchase agreement the Chinese have made with a Western country, may be intended to increase the marketability of their newest fighter, the F-8II, on the international market. The price of the basic air frame is relatively low by international standards, but foreign purchasers generally want Western avionics, the electronic systems that control an aircraft's armaments and navigation. The Chinese already are selling on the world market armored personnel carriers developed with the technical assistance of British and American firms. China may also acquire the technology to produce an older model U.S. torpedo which the Chinese hope to produce and sell to third countries. Even with their own limited domestic technology the Chinese have already emerged in recent years as the fifth largest supplier of arms on the international market with sales estimated at 2 billion U.S. dollars in 1985.

Finally, and perhaps most important, the United States' preoccupation with the potential security relationship with China has diverted our attention from more promising opportunities. China's domestic reforms and increasingly outward economic orientation create the possibility of China playing a positive economic role in Northeast Asia. Despite the progress that has been made, outlined in the opening pages of this study, U.S. policy could help to create an even more dynamic pattern of trade within Northeast Asia.

Proposed U.S. Policy Initiatives

First, the United States should encourage Taiwan to open direct trade with the People's Republic of China. The policy of the Nationalist party to prohibit direct trade is an impediment to a growing trade relationship. Moreover, since Hong Kong traditionally has been Taiwan's third largest export market, the current prohibition on direct trade will not be a viable policy once Hong Kong reverts to Chinese sovereignty in 1997. Taiwan's remarkable performance in international trade over more than than three decades should provide the self-confidence necessary for allowing direct trade. United States support of businessmen in Taiwan who have been discreetly pressing the government for liberalized trade could lead to the sanction of direct trade perhaps leading to other forms of economic cooperation between Taiwan and China in the future.

Second, the United States must begin to formulate a realistic strategy to deal with the increasing role of the Soviet Union in East Asia. To date our strategy has focused primarily on building up our naval forces in the Pacific region in an attempt to maintain superiority over a growing Soviet military presence in the area. But we have as yet not recognized that the Soviets have legitimate interests in East Asia. Given the prospect of increased Sino-Soviet cooperation and possible three way cooperation among China, Japan and the Soviet Union to exploit natural resources in Siberia, the U.S. policy of directing unrelenting criticism of Soviet aims in East Asia seems increasingly incongruous to other states in the region.

Third, the United States should be more supportive of China's efforts to get North Korea to open its economy to the West. The North Koreans, with Chinese encouragement and support, did promulgate a joint venture law in September 1984 to attract foreign investment and technology. It is modeled on the Chinese joint venture law of 1979 but in some respects is more favorable to foreign investors, perhaps reflecting North Korea's tentative desire to diversify its patterns of trade and sources of capital. To date the United States has refused to work directly with the Chinese to encourage the North Koreans to alter their trade and development policies—preferring instead the much more cautious development of what are referred to as "cross-contacts", a process in which the United States allows certain modest cultural exchanges with North Korea and the Chinese pursue contacts with the South.

While it is not clear how prepared the North Korean leadership is to open its economy to the outside world, U.S. policy should take that as a long-term objective for the benefits we would derive. Any reduction in the degree of insularity of the North Korean leadership and reduction in its very predominant dependence on the Soviet Union for economic aid and trade would be of substantial direct benefit to the United States.

Moreover, drawing North Korea into the world economic system would have the effect of breaking down the remaining barriers to expanded intraregional trade in Northeast Asia. It would lead to direct trade between North and South Korea, which in turn, would pave the way for formal trade ties between China and South Korea—the North Koreans could hardly continue to complain about China's trade with the South if they had such a direct trade relationship themselves. This would also clear the way for the development of a trade relationship between the United States and North Korea and would probably lead to expanded trade between Japan and North Korea as well.

While the U.S. policy makers have been partially mesmerized by the prospect of significant military sales to China and have not taken appropriate steps to encourage new trade relationships in the region, they have also failed to devote sufficient resources to development of bilateral commercial relations and have been caught off guard by increased Sino-U.S. competition in third-country markets.

Competition in Third Country Markets

Competition between the United States and China in third-country markets was once thought to be an unlikely possibility given the huge disparities in the level of economic development and technological sophistication of the two countries. But the success of China's agricultural reforms and the resulting changes in its trade patterns in agricultural products have had major implications for the United States. Not only has the United States lost a market in China for several million tons of wheat annually, it has also lost large sales of food grains, corn and soybeans to Japan, South Korea and the Soviet Union because Chinese products have either in part or entirely replaced those previously purchased from the United States. In 1984 and 1985, for example, U.S. sales of corn to Japan fell by more than 2.5 million tons (almost 25 percent) due largely to increased sales by China, a not insignificant development since corn is the biggest single U.S. export to Japan.

Similarly, the United States has lost substantial sales of raw cotton to Japan, Taiwan and other nations because of tripling of Chinese cotton output between 1978 and 1985 and the resulting shifts in the pattern of trade. As recently as 1980 China was one of the largest purchasers of raw cotton on the international market, importing almost 900,000 metric tons, more than half of which was supplied by the United States. Beginning in 1983 China became an exporter of cotton. By 1985 exports rose to 350,000 metric tons of cotton, and in 1986 exports rose even further as China became the world's third largest cotton exporter after the United States and the Soviet Union.

China's coal exports also are growing rapidly, from 7.6 million tons in 1984 to a planned 16 million tons in 1987. Sales in the major markets, Japan, Hong Kong and Western Europe, place China in a position of increased competition with the United States. In short, like Japan in the 1920s, China is now becoming a significant factor in world markets for some important traded commodities. This will lead to friction in the bilateral relationship and to competition in third-country markets for a growing number of commodities.

The United States and Japan: Cooperation or Competition

Japan, not the United States, has reaped a major share of the benefits of China's growing international trade. Both the Japanese government and Japanese firms have taken a long-run strategic view of the China market and committed commensurate resources to its development. For example, Japanese producers of electronic goods began consumer-oriented advertising in China almost a decade ago when most Western countries thought that China would never be in the market for consumer durable goods.

The Japanese, through a variety of institutions, have developed significantly greater research capability than the United States on China's foreign trade and its domestic economy. As a result, Japanese firms are probably the best informed in the world about developments in the China market. The Japanese External Trade Organization, under the Ministry of International Trade and Industry, maintains a large research staff in its China section office in Tokyo, a liaison office in Beijing and a second China office in Shanghai. The quasi-private Japan-China Association on Economy and Trade also maintains offices in China and a research program in Tokyo. Finally, longer-term research on China's economy undertaken by organizations such as the Institute of Developing Economies is supported by the Japanese government. During the period when the Japanese have done more to support economic data gathering and research on China, including the purchase of large-scale data sets from China that are not available in the United States, the U.S. government eliminated the only government office with the capacity for sustained, indepth research on the Chinese economy—the China Branch of the Office of Economic Research of the Central Intelligence Agency.

Similarly, Japanese firms have taken a longer-term view of the China market as compared to their U.S. counterparts. Japanese firms, for example, maintain five times more resident representative offices in China than do American firms. And whereas most U.S. firm offices are located in Beijing, the Japanese firms are widely distributed geographically. They have as many representatives in Shanghai as do U.S. firms in all of China, but they also maintain offices in Qingdao, Nanjing, Fuzhou and even in distant Xinjiang.

In the late 1970s the Japanese government proposed a joint U.S.-Japan effort to facilitate China's modernization. It was based on a broad vision of the potential contribution that China might make to economic growth and political stability not only in East Asia but in the world as a whole. The United States government, while sharing the positive view of China's potential, chose not to explore the cooperative program that the Japanese sought for China's economic development. Instead the United States chose to emphasize individual bilateral rather than coordinated multilateral policy, perhaps in part because of the implicit premise that unlike Sino-Japanese relations, Sino-American relations would include a significant military component. Also, American policy was predicated on the view that the United States was the most logical, if not the only, source for much of the technology that China sought for its modernization. That was particularly the case for offshore oil development whose scale was anticipated at the time to be so great that it was a foregone conclusion that the U.S. based major multinational oil companies would be the major actors.

In part, too, the United States' choice was consistent with our broader policy of minimizing Japan's military role in East Asia based on the belief that Japan's contribution to global peace would be best achieved through increasing its economic aid and trade relations in the region. The result has been that the Japanese have focused their energies on economic relations in the region while the United States has borne most, if not quite all, of the burden of security in the region.

From the perspective of the mid-1980s the situation has changed somewhat. The development of offshore oil has been very disappointing—only very modest deposits have been discovered, and offshore oil production in 1986 was only 375,000 tons, a tiny fraction of China's total petroleum output. Ironically the most important source of offshore oil was the Chengbei field, developed with the cooperation of the Japanese. Not only has large scale offshore petroleum development been relatively unsuccessful thus far, but the United States has met increased foreign competition or other setbacks in other areas which were once thought to be natural areas for cooperation. The Reagan administration, for example, expended considerable political capital to secure Senate approval of a bilateral nuclear agreement with China which, it was claimed, would lead to multibillion dollar sales of nuclear power generation equipment. But the Chinese plans for further nuclear power development have been shelved, and the prospect for U.S. sales has dimmed considerably. Similarly in many other sectors Japanese firms have emerged as unexpectedly strong competitors. Even in areas where U.S. firms may be competitive the absence of U.S. government supported financing may make large scale sales problematic.

The increasingly competitive economic environment in the China market and China's shift toward a more equidistant posture vis-à-vis the United States and the Soviet Union have two important implications for United States policy in Northeast Asia. First, the focus of our bilateral relations with China should be redirected to place greater emphasis on economic and trade matters. Second, to the extent the United States desires increased regional military cooperation to counter growing Soviet military forces in the region the logical partner for that increased role would be Japan, not the People's Republic of China.

Suggested Reading

Japan External Trade Organization, "China Newsletter," Tokyo, bimonthly.

Keidel, Albert, editor, "China Economic Letter," Washington, DC: Rock Creek Research, semimonthly.

Lee, Chae-Jin, *China and Japan: New Economic Diplomacy*, Stanford, CA: Hoover Institution Press, 1984.

Lincoln, Edward J., *Japan's Economic Role in Northeast Asia*, New York: The Asia Society, and Lanham, MD: University Press of America, 1987.

Perkins, Dwight H., *China: Asia's Next Economic Giant*, Seattle: University of Washington Press, 1986.

Scalapino, Robert A., *Major Power Relations in Northeast Asia*, New York: The Asia Society, and Lanham, MD: University Press of America, 1986.

Whiting, Allen, *Siberian Development and East Asia: Threat or Promise*, Stanford, CA: Stanford University Press, 1981.

About the Author

Nicholas R. Lardy is currently Chairman of the China Program and Professor of International Studies at the Jackson School of International Studies, University of Washington, Seattle. Professor Lardy served as Associate Professor of Economics at Yale University (1979-1983) where he was also Assistant Director of the Economic Growth Center (1979-1982), and Assistant Professor of Economics (1975-1979). Professor Lardy received his M.A. and Ph.D. in economics from the University of Michigan (1975). His major publications include: *Economic Growth and Distribution in China* (1978); *Chen Yun's Strategy for China's Development: A Non-Maoist Alternative*, ed. (1983); and *Agriculture in China's Modern Economic Development* (1983).